# AWS for Public and Private Sectors

## Cloud Computing Architecture for Government and Business

Bradley Fowler

Apress®

*AWS for Public and Private Sectors: Cloud Computing Architecture for Government and Business*

Bradley Fowler
Canton, MI, USA

ISBN-13 (pbk): 978-1-4842-9047-7          ISBN-13 (electronic): 978-1-4842-9048-4
https://doi.org/10.1007/978-1-4842-9048-4

Managing Director, Apress Media LLC: Welmoed Spahr
Acquisitions Editor: Celestin Suresh John
Development Editor: James Markham
Coordinating Editor: Mark Powers

Cover designed by eStudioCalamar
Cover image by Steve Johnson on Unsplash (www.unsplash.com)

Distributed to the book trade worldwide by Apress Media, LLC, 1 New York Plaza, New York, NY 10004, U.S.A. Phone 1-800-SPRINGER, fax (201) 348-4505, e-mail orders-ny@springer-sbm.com, or visit www.springeronline.com. Apress Media, LLC is a California LLC and the sole member (owner) is Springer Science + Business Media Finance Inc (SSBM Finance Inc). SSBM Finance Inc is a **Delaware** corporation.

For information on translations, please e-mail booktranslations@springernature.com; for reprint, paperback, or audio rights, please e-mail bookpermissions@springernature.com.

Apress titles may be purchased in bulk for academic, corporate, or promotional use. eBook versions and licenses are also available for most titles. For more information, reference our Print and eBook Bulk Sales web page at http://www.apress.com/bulk-sales.

Any source code or other supplementary material referenced by the author in this book is available to readers on GitHub (https://github.com/Apress). For more detailed information, please visit http://www.apress.com/source-code.

Printed on acid-free paper

# Table of Contents

# About the Author

**Bradley Fowler** earned a Master of Science in Cloud Computing Architecture from the University of Maryland Global Campus *cum laude*, where he spent 18 months applying his knowledge in cloud computing architecture with BallotOnline global voting systems as acting Chief Cloud Architect. Bradley also earned a Master of Public Policy in Cybersecurity Policy from the American Public University System *summa cum laude* and a Master of Science in Cybersecurity and a Master of Science in Managing Information Systems in Information Security Management, both from Bellevue University, both *summa cum laude*. Bradley also earned a Master of Arts in Teaching and Learning with Technology *summa cum laude* and a Bachelor of Arts in eMarketing *cum laude*, both from Ashford University, which is now the University of Arizona Global Campus. Bradley is completing dissertation research for a Doctor of Education in Educational Administration with California Coast University and completing a Doctor of Management in Information Systems and Technology at the University of Phoenix College of Doctoral Studies, as well as a PhD in Cybersecurity Leadership at Capitol Technology University.

Bradley is a member of the Golden Key International Honour Society, National Cybersecurity Alliance, and National Cybersecurity Student Association. He is a contributing writer for the National Security Policy and Analysis Organization and co-author of *Cybersecurity Public Policy: SWOT Analysis Conducted on 43 Countries*. Bradley's hobbies include weight training, roller skating, traveling, cooking, roller coasters, and writing fiction and nonfiction material – that is, books, articles, and scholarly conference papers.

# Acknowledgments

Dr. Shawn Khan was an inspiration to me during my learning opportunity at the University of Maryland Global Campus. It was helpful having him as my instructor; I only hoped we would have had the opportunity to work together on this book.

It is always challenging to overcome obstacles alone, but, Bruce, you have been a champion throughout the course of actions deployed to achieve the goals set to continue researching and developing training material that educates others. Thank you for your support.

The National Institute of Standards and Technology (NIST) – Having your publication series as guides to help make effective recommendations is important. Please do not stop revising and sharing these special publications that support both public and private sector entities.

The National Security Agency, thank you for staying the course and rendering quality control that deters cyberthreats that impact cloud infrastructures.

Amazon Web Services (AWS) – Without the ability to understand the various services required to operate an effective and efficient cloud virtual private infrastructure, I would not be able to share what I've learned. Thank you so much for the continued usage of AWS Management Console and AWS services for cloud computing architecture and automation.

Thank you, God, for my diligence to be an effective writer and researcher.

# Introduction

In today's progressive world, technology dependence impacts government, parliament, ministries, and civilians. The use of hardware, software, information systems, information technology, and cloud Software as a Service (SaaS), Infrastructure as a Service (IaaS), or Platform as a Service (PaaS) to operate, transmit, and store small and large information system databases has become a normal daily business and government operation. Therefore, it is important to understand what cloud computing architecture is. After all, cloud computing architecture offers consumers a return on investment while enabling consumers to effectively manage total cost of ownership (TCO) and monthly cost associated with services rendered by cloud computing service providers. In fact, due to the wide selection of cloud computing service providers, it is important to understand how to effectively evaluate cloud service providers (CSPs) to determine which service provider is reliable, capable, and trustworthy to provide secure services to host an enterprise's information assets. The service provider must also offer cloud consumers the ability to increase security of all cloud applications an enterprise will utilize to develop, store, and transmit information assets an enterprise needs to operate. This book will provide you information you need to understand why AWS is the best cloud service provider. This book will also help you understand AWS Service Level Agreements. After all, cloud consumers need to know how to assess all services their enterprise requires to effectively develop, store, transmit, and secure information assets in the cloud.

As you read this book, you will be introduced to strategies and recommendations that were deployed for BallotOnline, a global voting system service provider who sought to migrate their on-premises information system to the cloud. Utilizing BallotOnline as an example throughout this self-study guide will help you improve how you assess, develop, implement, manage, and update your enterprise information system into a cloud. In fact, you will acquire knowledge of AWS EC2 Instance. EC2 Instance is dynamic for applications integrated with tools and resources in twin proportions, that is, web servers and code databases. EC2 Instance multiple Instance types are measurable for different use cases. EC2 Instance types unite multiple tools and resources, including the Central Processing Unit (CPU), memory, storage, and network scalability, to enable flexibility as well as for electing a mixed model of resources. Each Instance type is available in multiple sizes and is scalable.

You will also learn about using a total cost of ownership calculator (see Notes), which Amazon Web Services (AWS) renders to help you understand how financial requirements for cloud computing architecture differ from the financial requirements for on-premises information systems and networks. In addition, you will gain knowledge about relevant security issues and cloud laws and policy the US Department of Commerce and the National Institute of Standards and Technology enacted to help reduce security risks associated with cloud services. The NIST stresses "a cloud consumer needs to analyze the risk associated with the adoption of a cloud-based solution for a particular information system, and plan for the risk treatment and risk control activities associated with the cloud-based operations of this system" [1].

Therefore, this book will help you acquire visibility into cloud services so you can effectively define your enterprise's cloud system as well as gain understanding on how to negotiate required risk treatment and risk control mitigations, prior to finalizing the SLA (Service Level Agreement). You will also gain knowledge about network engineering for cloud services, including Internet Protocol, packet switching, IP addressing, DNS, and IP routing. Furthermore, you will learn about Transmission Control Protocol (TCP), TCP connections, ensuring transport reliability, and TCP sliding windows as well as acquire understanding of the AWS migration environment and configuration of web services.

Next, you will acquire knowledge about the advantages and disadvantages of AWS S3 and AWS Glacier service packs. This book provides strategies to evaluate, plan, develop, implement, and manage such services acquired by Amazon Web Services. Furthermore, you will increase your knowledge about data backup and archiving to the cloud using AWS CloudWatch monitoring. Then, you will acquire information about AWS OpsWorks. OpsWorks enables you to use Chef or Puppet to automate how servers are configured, deployed, and managed, including backup and archiving across your enterprise's Amazon EC2 Instances or on-premises compute environments [2].

Additionally, you will be introduced to two basic approaches to data migration: lift and shift and create new. Lift and shift involves extracting current replicated applications in the cloud without modifying them, to enable end users to migrate their existing servers, including the data, while create new involves creating a new server in the cloud as necessary and only mirroring the data to the cloud. And last but equally important are AWS Trusted Advisor and AWS Systems Manager. Learning how to utilize these tools will help you prepare an application comparison.

# List of Abbreviations

API – Application Programming Interface

SDK – Software Development Kit

CLI – Command Line Interface

IAM – Identity and Access Management

ENISA – European Network and Information Security Agency

EU – European Union

CDK – Cloud Development Kit

IDE – Integrated Development Environment

vCPU – Virtual Central Processing Unit

VM – Virtual Machine

ACL – Access Control List

# CHAPTER 1

# Cloud Services and Technologies

**Learning Objectives**

> Gain an understanding of cloud Software as a Service.
>
> Distinguish cloud service provider reliability.
>
> Be able to effectively evaluate cloud services to meet your organizational needs.
>
> Understand why cloud service providers must be compliant with federal laws and regulations.

Deciding to upgrade an on-premises system to cloud infrastructure requires understanding what services and products you will need to create a smooth upgrade from a physical hardware system to a virtual private cloud (VPC). Learning how to assess which service provider can meet the needs of your enterprise is extremely important. In this chapter, you will gain understanding about strategies and develop plans previously assessed, developed, and implemented on behalf of BallotOnline during their transition to a cloud business system. The BallotOnline experience will also enable you to understand how to effectively manage your own enterprise information system in the cloud and control the cost to do so.

In fact, you will gain information that will help you define the total cost of ownership, using a total cost of ownership (TCO) calculator, offered by Amazon Web Services (AWS) and Microsoft Azure. After all, financial requirements for cloud computing will differ greatly industry by industry. Furthermore, cloud computing cost can shift budgets to a pure operating expense model, whereas traditional on-premises computing infrastructure requires capital and operating expense allocations.

© Bradley Fowler 2023
B. Fowler, *AWS for Public and Private Sectors*, https://doi.org/10.1007/978-1-4842-9048-4_1

# Establishing the Framework

Amazon Web Services (AWS) TCO also enables you to utilize Amazon Aurora, which is MySQL-compatible and designed for the cloud as well as combines performance and availability of traditional enterprise databases with a simple cost-effectiveness usage of open source databases [1]. When I discovered the value of integrating the data needed for BallotOnline transition, such as understanding the description of the current estimated funding allocation for the BallotOnline information system IT budget, I discovered that configuring the AWS Management Console dashboard required me to select a region as well as select the number of nodes to be modified [2]. I also discovered I needed to know how to select the correct Instance class BallotOnline needed as well as how to configure the Instance. Thus, I configured BallotOnline settings as follows: db.t2.medium; the v2CPU (Central Processing Unit) was set at (2); the Memory was set at 4 GB; the Network Performance was set at Low to Moderate. You will also need to set your Instance Family, which for BallotOnline was designated as General Purpose, and the pricing model was selected for On-Demand. Next, you will need to add the current database storage, which for BallotOnline was 400 database servers with 64 GB RAM (Random Access Memory), which equaled 25,600 GB. Of course, the configuration settings for your enterprise will differ greatly.

Once the configuration is set, it is easy to request a system calculation. Doing so will enable you to acquire understanding of the monthly cost for services relied on. For BallotOnline, the monthly calculation cost was $4,326.34 or $ 51,916.08 annually. Figure 1-1 provides a proof of concept.

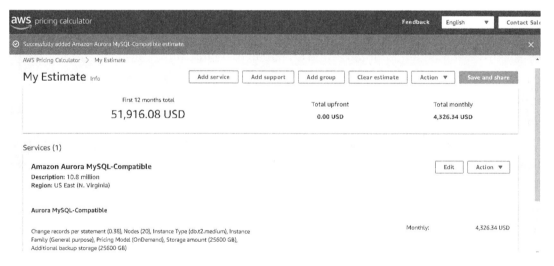

***Figure 1-1.*** *Requesting a system calculation*

During this process of calculating your system needs, you will be asked to provide information regarding the current database your enterprise utilizes. BallotOnline was utilizing Microsoft SQL Server, and their current License setting was Enterprise. The Environment setting is Physical, and the operating system is Windows. The operating system license is Datacenter. You will also be asked to provide information about your enterprise current storage allocation. Next, you will be required to add the total number of gigabytes from the network bandwidth your enterprise currently consumes with its on-premises system. Additionally, you will be asked about the electricity cost, that is, price per kWh (kilowatt-hour). Figures 1-2 through 1-6 provide proofs of concept.

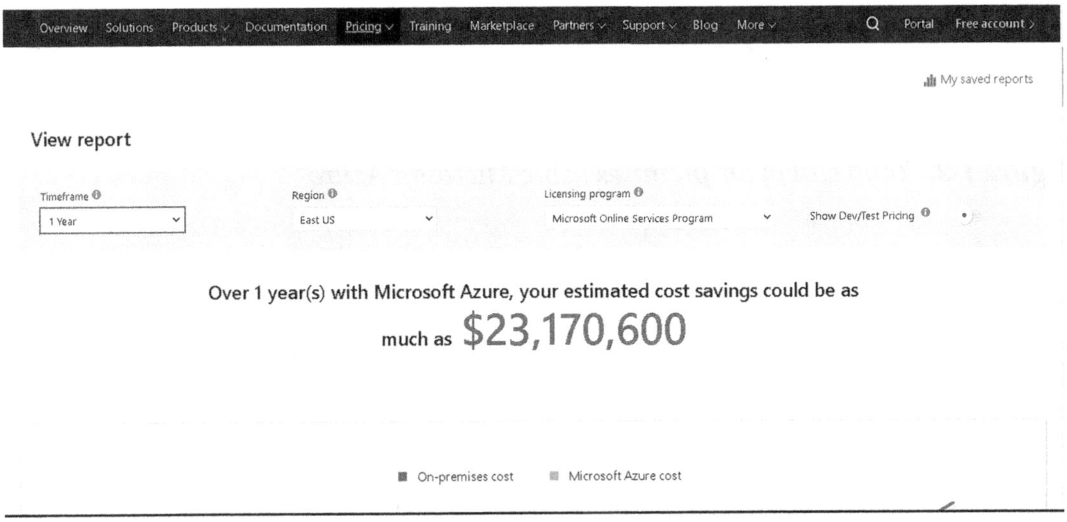

**Figure 1-2.** *Results of calculation for estimated cost*

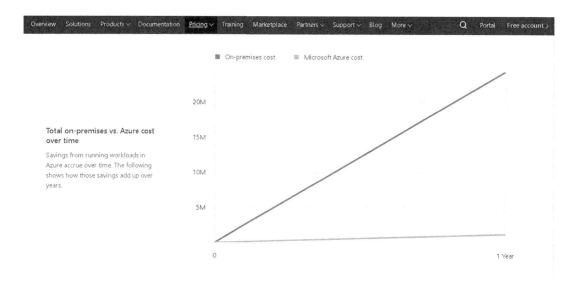

**Figure 1-3.** *Total cost of on-premises using Microsoft Azure*

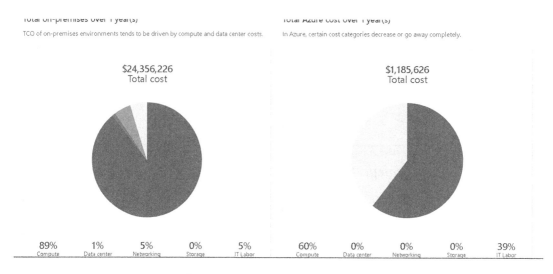

**Figure 1-4.** *Comparison of total costs over 1 year*

**Figure 1-5.** *Total on-premises cost*

## $24,356,226
Cost over 1 year(s)

## $1,185,626
Cost over 1 year(s)

On-premises cost breakdown summary

| Category | Cost |
|---|---|
| Compute | $21,620,888.00 |
|   Hardware | $1,126,080.00 |
|   Software | $6,155,000.00 |
|   Electricity | $98,208.00 |
|   Database | $14,241,600.00 |
| Data Center | $312,886.62 |
| Networking | $1,302,066.30 |
| Storage | $385.28 |
| IT Labor | $1,120,000.00 |
| **Total** | **$24,356,226.00** |

Azure cost breakdown summary

| Category | Cost |
|---|---|
| Compute | $715,056.00 |
| Data Center | $0.00 |
| Networking | $3,072.00 |
| Storage | $831.12 |
| IT Labor | $466,666.90 |
| **Total** | **$1,185,626.00** |

**Figure 1-6.** *On-premises cost evaluation*

As conveyed, these figures are estimates for BallotOnline delivery of service, both monthly and annually. After evaluating these figures, it clearly can be seen that upgrading from your current on-premises system to a cloud architecture can reduce your enterprise budget cost. Keep in mind budget evaluations are essential to determining how to assess an amount the enterprise is willing to invest in utilizing cloud services (SaaS), infrastructure (IaaS), or platforms (PaaS).

Next, you will need to understand the value of functional and nonfunctional requirements, including critical IT requirements relating to data storage. Having this knowledge will also enable you to understand that functional requirements specify the behavior of a system and help determine what the system should effectively do. Possessing this information prior to the acquisition of development is key to allocating sufficient funding to begin designating budget funding toward creating a reliable system. In addition, understanding nonfunctional requirements, which help convey how the system supports the functional requirements, is important. This provides clarity regarding the methodologies of verification of functional requirements and includes additional requirements not included within the functional requirements.

# Critical IT Requirements Related to Data Storage

Critical IT requirements relating to data storage include concerns of policy and information security management. This includes encryption, decryption, and audit trails. Encryption is important because it conceals data content in a cipher language that cannot be decrypted unless the receiver has the public key to decrypt the message. Decryption occurs when the receiver opens the file to read the content in plain-text format. Audit trails envelope records of system activity, that is, data on the information system, processes, application processes, and all user activities that must be effectively managed.

Additionally important is conducting a risk assessment and developing and maintaining a compliance report. The National Institute of Standards and Technology recommended guidelines to help you identify the most appropriate guidelines for managing risks and provide details about the best approach to risk management. The importance of risk and compliance assessment in cloud adoption is outlined by the National Institute of Standards and Technology (NIST), who explains that "a cloud consumer needs to analyze the risk associated with the adoption of a cloud-based solution for a particular information system, and plan for the risk treatment and risk control activities associated with the cloud-based operations of this system" [3]. It is recommended that cloud consumers gain a clear perspective of the cloud ecosystem that hosts the operations of the cloud-based information system.

# Risk Analysis

With the integration of cloud computing architecture, there are risks that must be assessed to determine the impact such risks will have on your daily business operations. This encompasses compute power, networking, storage, as well as an interface for end users to access the virtualized resources. Each virtual resource mirrors the physical infrastructure, including networking, compute, and storage components. Utilizing cloud computing and storage infrastructure reduces cost, provides scalability, and delivers greater flexibility.

**Advantages of cloud computing architecture**

- Lowers dependency on support and hardware

- Accessibility anytime, anywhere

- Scalability

- Reduces budget spending

- Provides increased security

**Disadvantages of cloud computing architecture**

- Data can be modified.

- Data can be leaked.

Thus, to effectively secure the cloud computing architecture selected for BallotOnline, it was essential to conduct a risk analysis using a risk management matrix. You may find it beneficial to conduct your own risk analysis. Figure 1-7 provides a risk management matrix that was designed for BallotOnline [4].

The likelyhood of security risk factors increases with the usage of technology that host information developed and relied upon by any enterprise.

The chart below conveys levels of security concerns when data is at rest, in transmission, and in usage. A lack of security protocol can increase the level of risk associated with data that is not effectively secured.

| Data at rest | Data in transmission | Data in usage |
|---|---|---|
| High risk | High risk | High risk |
| Medium risk | Medium risk | Medium risk |
| Low risk | Low risk | Low risk |

***Figure 1-7.*** *Risk management matrix*

This risk management matrix reports that when data is at rest, the risk can measure high, medium, or low. The level of security implemented for data at rest determines the risk associated with that data. When data is at rest in the cloud, it can be secured by controlled access authorization, which limits the number of personnel who have access to the data. The same applies to data in transmission and data in usage. Security approaches to prevent unauthorized access to data typically include multi-factor log-in credentials consisting of username and password. A thorough approach to defining a risk analysis is utilizing a risk factor table, which includes a date of the risk discovery, cause of the risk factor, type of risk management deployed, consequences of the risk discovered, full risk details, and risk owner or person(s) responsible for the risk exposure and exploitation, as well as the risk probability, that is, likely, unlikely, or very likely; the impact of the risk, that is, minor, moderately, or major; and a risk score, that is, acceptable risk medium or low and unacceptable risk high or extremely high. This also includes a response action type – that is, avoid, transfer, mitigate, or accept. Thus, it is essential to utilize these response actions to mitigate issues and deploy methodologies to effectively deter future risks.

# Risk Management Guidelines

When evaluating the risk associated with cloud computing architecture, you must consider all federal recommendations and guidelines. To effectively secure the cloud database, the US Department of Defense, the National Institute of Standards and Technology, and the Industry Standard Organization (ISO) have developed guidelines as precautionary tools of security, both for public and private sector enterprises, organizations, academia, and nonprofits. Due to the services and products BallotOnline offers and will be offering via its cloud infrastructure, BallotOnline was required to align its information security policy with ISO 27001 because this enables BallotOnline to "plan for information security risk and the treatment of the risk" [5]. In fact, ISO 27001 makes it a requirement to develop, implement, manage, and improve information security management systems as well as address the requirements for assessing and mitigating information security risks. Thus, it is important you have knowledge of the federal recommendations and guidelines published under the NIST SP 800 series to decrease liabilities or civil or criminal charges that could be brought against your enterprise for violating a consumer's privacy and for not effectively securing consumers' data in your virtual private cloud. For instance, NIST SP 800-144 provides guidelines on security and privacy in public cloud computing. Aligning your enterprise cloud security and privacy policy with the National Institute of Standards and Technology helps you define a risk management approach that can be updated as needed and align with the needs of the enterprise. This includes implementing steps, such as categorizing information systems and selecting, implementing, assessing, authorizing, and monitoring security controls.

# Potential Privacy Issues and Mitigation Measures

Since BallotOnline is a global enterprise, it is required BallotOnline adhere to global privacy laws that were recently enacted by the European Commission, including the General Data Protection Regulation (GDPR). Enacted in 2018, the GDPR was passed to increase the protection of personal data and to ensure all individuals have the right to privacy via new data protection, security, and compliance requirements. This law was enacted to create "a privacy by default" approach to secure sensitive data. The GDPR encompasses six key components:

- Fairness and lawfulness

- Purpose limitation

- Data minimization

- Accuracy

- Storage limitation

- Integrity and confidentiality

In addition, the US National Security Agency shares new regulations on cloud computing risk mitigation measures that should be adhered to. For instance, it is recommended "cloud customers have a critical role in mitigating misconfiguration and poor access control, but can also take actions to protect cloud resources from the exploitation of shared tenancy and supply chain vulnerabilities" [6]. Because cloud service providers (CSPs) deploy services differently, there are different approaches to securing data hosted by the cloud. The National Security Agency conveys that there are four key components that must be considered when acquiring services from a cloud service provider, such as Identity and Access Management, which manages customers' ability to protect accessibility to their data housed in the cloud as well as manage the cloud service provider's access to back-end cloud resources [7]. The NSA also recommends enforcement of auditing as a method of protecting cloud customer data.

Also invaluable is computing – that is, virtualization and containerization, networking, and storage. Thus, the NSA recommends using cloud services that enable encryption and key management control. As conveyed previously, encrypting data will provide a security layer that conceals information both at rest and in transmission. Enabling a key management system will provide limited access to the data housed in the cloud environment and enable better accountability measures to assess who accesses the data, when, where, and how.

Additional privacy issues include protection of end users' data. In fact, each state your enterprise conducts business operations in may have its own laws regarding the storage and usage of customer data. For instance, the state of California passed the Consumer Privacy Act (CPA) and the Privacy Rights Act (PRA). These two laws are vital to protecting the data of California residents. Many other states have similar laws, such as Maine, Maryland, Massachusetts, Nevada, New Jersey, New York, Oregon, Texas, Virginia, and Washington. There are additional laws that should be assessed, such as the Payment Card Industry (PCI) Data Security Standard and the Federal Information Security Management Act (FISMA). Staying current with enacted laws helps reduce liabilities your enterprise may face when consumers feel their data is being housed without effective privacy protections.

# Relevant Security Issues

There are several relevant security issues encompassed in cloud computing architecture, for instance, "security concerns relating to risk areas – i.e., external data storage, dependency on the "public" Internet, lack of control, multi-tenancy and integration with internal security" [8]. Compared with traditional technologies, the cloud has several unique features such as scalability as well as resources belonging to cloud providers that are completely distributed, heterogeneous, and virtualized. When cloud service providers (CSPs) do not include security such as encryption, firewalls, and intrusion detection, security of end users' data is left up to the service account owner. This makes your enterprise responsible for making sure access to the cloud and all your data stored in the cloud is secure and protected effectively. In fact, because of the three cloud models – Software as a Service (SaaS), Infrastructure as a Service (IaaS), and Platform as a Service (PaaS) – it is important to understand what steps should be deployed to secure each model once it is determined what cloud service provider best serves the needs of your enterprise. With Software as a Service, the burden of security is on the cloud service provider. With Infrastructure as a Service (IaaS), there is increased tenant or customer control over security. Platform as a Service (PaaS) delivers increased extensibility at the cost of greater customer control.

Next, there are security issues relating to the physical data security center, which include securing access and resiliency of facilities. Concerns also include account access security and issues making sure all data housed in a cloud or physical server is secure, aligned with security policy and regulations recommendations from the US Department of Commerce, the National Institute of Standards and Technology, the US Department of Homeland Security, the National Security Agency, and the White House, if you are operating within the United States. If you are operating outside the United States, it is essential to have knowledge of the laws in whatever country or countries your enterprise will be conducting virtual cloud business in.

No matter what model of cloud service you elect, deployment of effective security is required and should always encompass primary security controls – for example, multi-factor authentication log-in, intrusion detection, firewalls, and least privileges. Therefore, security policies should be developed and implemented, and all personnel must be trained and made aware of the role and responsibility they have in alignment with the implementation and continued effectiveness of all policies. Otherwise, you leave an open gateway of vulnerabilities that can be exploited, especially when human error is involved. In addition, there are concerns of system updates and backups that should be conducted daily. This is done to reduce vulnerabilities and deter unauthorized access to sensitive components enveloped in the system.

# Applicable Laws and Regulations

There are countless applicable laws and regulations to align your enterprise security efforts and policy with. Neglecting to do so can be costly and create liabilities that can be avoided. For instance, there are intellectual property laws that should be evaluated and considered, especially those enacted worldwide. Intellectual property includes trademarks, copyright, patents, and industrial design rights and grants legal protection to the creator of original works, such as music, motion pictures, literature, designs, inventions, words, slogans, phrases, and symbols, from misappropriation by others. Therefore, owners of intellectual property assets must deploy safeguards and security measures to protect such from piracy, infringement, counterfeiting, and theft. The World Intellectual Property Organization (WIPO) establishes the legitimate rights that relate to artistic and scientific works, performances of performing artists, phonograms and broadcasts, human inventions, scientific discoveries, industrial developments, trademarks, and commercial names. Having knowledge of this information is essential. The following is a compiled list of laws and regulations that should be researched and, if applicable, be implemented and aligned with all security policies developed for your enterprise virtual cloud business operations. Keep in mind it is essential to always conduct effective research to understand the laws and regulations applicable to your enterprise needs.

**Applicable laws**

- Berne Convention for the Protection of Literary and Artistic Works, 1886

- WIPO Copyright Treaty, 1996

- WIPO Performances and Phonograms Treaty, 1996

- Cloud computing law (see details in the following)

*In the case of cloud computing applications, it is the overall design of the user interface that implements the features and functionalities from which users can benefit. All data and content stored in the cloud can only be accessed through the interface provided by the cloud provider, which specifically determines the way users are entitled to interact with them, regardless of their legal status. Therefore, it could be said that, in the context of cloud computing, "the user interface is law."* [9]

- Cyberspace law (see details in the following)

  Cyberlaws encompass international treaties that must be acknowledged and adhered to. Thus, it is imperative to effectively research all cloud hosting agreement details, such as scope of processing, subcontractors, deletion of data, data security measure, localization of data, restitution of data, and audits.

- Sarbanes-Oxley Act

- Customs Trade Partnership Against Terrorism (CTPAT)

- Federal Rules of Civil Procedure

- Federal Information Security Management Act

- North American Electric Reliability Corp. (NERC) standards

- Title 21 of the Code of Federal Regulations (21 CFR Part 11) – Electronic Records

- California Consumer Privacy Act (CCPA)

- California Privacy Rights Act (CPRA)

- Maine Act to Protect the Privacy of Online Consumer Information

- Maryland Personal Information Protection Act – Security Breach Notification Requirements – Modifications (House Bill 1154)

- Massachusetts 201 CMR 17 (a.k.a. Mass Data Protection Law)

- Personal Information Protection and Electronic Documents Act (PIPED Act, or PIPEDA) – Canada

- Law on the Protection of Personal Data Held by Private Parties – Mexico

- General Data Protection Regulation (GDPR)

**List of high-level policies**

NIST SP 500-291 Cloud Computing Standards Roadmap

NIST SP 800-144 Guidelines on Security and Privacy in Public Cloud Computing

NIST SP 800-181 Workforce Framework for Cybersecurity (NICE Framework)

NIST SP 500-169 Executive Guide to the Protection of Information Resources

NIST SP 800-14 Generally Accepted Principles and Practices for Securing Information Technology Systems

NIST SP 800-12 Introduction to Information Security

NIST SP 800-18 Guide for Developing Security Plans for Federal Information Systems

NIST SP 800-30 Guide for Conducting Risk Assessments

NIST SP 800-53 Security and Privacy Controls for Information Systems and Organizations

ISO 27000 series

ISO 27001

ISO 27002

US Patent and Trademark Office laws

US copyright laws

World Intellectual Property Organization law

Americans with Disabilities Act

**List of high-level education and training programs**

SANS Institute (www.sans.org)

National Institute of Standards and Technology (www.nist.gov/itl/applied-cybersecurity/nice/resources/online-learning-content)

US Election Assistance Commission (www.eac.gov/sites/default/files/eac_assets/1/28/EducatingVoters[3]-508 Compliant.pdf)

**Relationships between the two components of the program** – that is, communication channels and dependencies

- Email

- Fax

- Telecommunication

- Webinars

- Video Conferencing – for example, Microsoft Teams, Cisco Webex

**Enforcement mechanisms**

- Policy

- State and federal laws and regulations

- Awareness training

- Data encryption

- Biometrics

- Multi-factor authentication

**Monitoring and audit mechanisms**

- Continuous Monitoring (CM)

- Continuous Auditing (CA)

- US Environmental Protection Agency

Policy compliance issues must be managed by investigating the cause and effects as well as outcomes of noncompliance matters. This includes increasing penalties for noncompliant personnel, such as probationary periods, temporary suspension, or termination. Legal noncompliance can result in criminal and civil actions. Corporate noncompliance can also result in criminal and civil actions as well as fines. Thus, effective personnel awareness training should be developed by human resources, the chief information security officer (CISO), technical officers, and stakeholders, who will devise effective methods to regulate noncompliance concerns.

Risk assessments are handled through investigations to determine the issues enveloped in each circumstance and assess damages, if any. It is best to provide your enterprise executive members and stakeholders a thorough report evaluating cloud architecture services rendered by Amazon Web Services (AWS) and Microsoft Azure. Developing this report can support your enterprise initiative in acquiring clarity on the services provided by these two service providers. This report will also enable your enterprise to understand relevant risks associated with integrating the current IT trends in a cloud computing architecture and provide information about the policies associated with securing the information assets stored in the cloud architecture.

# Comparison of AWS and Microsoft Azure Architecture Deployments

Trends in cloud computing, such as virtualization, components of IT systems are increasingly defined by means of software, which often transitions into the introduction of more "software-defined" areas, from software-defined networking (SDN) and software-defined storage (SDS) to virtualizing all aspects of cloud data centers (software-defined data center [SDDC]) [10]. Furthermore, an increased usage of "everything as a service" (XaaS) now combines IaaS (Infrastructure as a Service), PaaS (Platform as a Service), and SaaS (Software as a Service). Additional trends such as hybrid cloud delivery models are becoming widely utilized.

Cloud deployment components are rendered in virtualized environments managed by software, there is limited freedom of determining the deployment of cloud reference models, which suggest recommendations to design solutions for typical elements of cloud services. This includes resource and service deployment and management, security, privacy, etc. In fact, a reference architecture (RA) for the cloud is a generic, high-level conceptual model facilitating the comprehension of cloud computing operational intricacies. However, the reference architecture does not represent the system architecture of a specific cloud computing system. Instead, this tool describes, discusses, and develops a system-specific architecture using a common framework for reference [11]. Since most components of cloud deployment are implemented in a virtualized environment managed by software, you will need to define the number of virtual servers required and determine the configurations as well as modify those configurations as needed. Furthermore, you will need to define the virtual local area networks (LANs) and subnets and put servers within such to implement network security configurations.

Your enterprise is responsible for administering the data in the database services. This requires your enterprise to give the database administrator direct access to the enterprise cloud database. To increase security in accessing the enterprise cloud requires limiting who has access privileges. Security should also include security zones. This enables your enterprise to be responsible for its proprietary data storage solutions. However, the service provider will only manage the server, not the database. Furthermore, increased-security zones include virtual private networks (VPNs) and private virtual local area networks, which limit who can access the network. Ideally, this is managed by the service provider, even though your enterprise will be able to access the service provider via its network, making this a hybrid model. Load balancing, auto-scaling, and database replication are services that encompass cloud architectures. These tools are scalable and enable your enterprise to determine what degree of scalability is needed based on the number of servers within the group, images which the servers are provisioned as well as be based on calendar and/or utilized based on network, bandwidth, CPU, or memory within the servers.

Meanwhile, fault tolerance and high availability are beneficial when a situation occurs that may impede on the consistency of cloud services. Fault tolerance and high availability assure that no matter what happens, the cloud services will not be impacted. After all, applications and databases are replicated and relocated to geographical locations to assure quick accessibility from remote locations. Doing so enables assurance of adhering to local government regulations and policy regarding data privacy.

Of course, with any form of outsourced service, your enterprise needs to have a team of experts who are knowledgeable of the facts and understand what needs to be done whenever an issue occurs. This means staying current in industry trends to take charge and deploy mitigation strategies that will combat potential risks and vulnerabilities. Even though, AWS shares its security methods and policy to assure security that encompasses the services of cloud applications deployed, your enterprise needs to implement effective management and leadership from those responsible for managing the enterprise's cloud service applications.

AWS offers tutorials that provide a step-by-step approach to developing applets and testing their efficiency. Relying on these services will help you learn how easy it is to create a sample app and follow along with the instructions to achieve the end goal.

Furthermore, it is invaluable to deploy effective training for all personnel who utilize technology to conduct daily operations and provide services on behalf of your enterprise. Doing so helps decrease any chance of liabilities that impact budget spending. One common issue that increases budget spending is human error, which results in vulnerabilities that impact the information system and/or cloud services personnel have access to and/or engages with. Thus, it is recommended to assess the enterprise current position with an external analysis. Doing so requires a strategic analysis that analyzes both internal and external environments. I recommended using Porter's Five Forces model. "While the five-force model was originally developed to assess industry attractiveness, in practice the model is often used to assess a specific firm's external environment" [12]. The first phase of the model is the degree of existing rivalry. "The number and relative size of competitors will shape the nature of rivalry" [13]. Next concern is threats of potential entrants, which are influenced by the likelihood the industry draws new entrants into the industry that replicate the services rendered to end users. The bargaining power of suppliers focuses on the degree to which an enterprise relies on AWS or Azure, to influence its ability to negotiate good terms. There is also the bargaining power of buyers, which aligns with the bargaining power of suppliers.

Next, having support for application migration and monitoring is important. For instance, Azure's native monitoring service, Azure Monitor, is equivalent to Amazon CloudWatch and both cloud services consolidate massive amounts of data from cloud and on-premises sources as well as provide visualization and analysis and allow users to respond to issues quickly and support a strong ecosystem of third-party solutions [14], Azure Monitor provides users with full observability into their cloud and on-premises environments, collecting and analyzing data from a variety of sources before storing the information to be later optimized for cost and performance.

# Comparison of Ease of Deployment

Furthermore, your enterprise "business needs drive cloud infrastructure choices, though what seems like a cost issue is often rooted in highly specific technical factors. Ease of use for a particular workload, for example, may vary depending on deployment on AWS or Azure. There could be a financial difference in the workload's administrative overhead as a result. Nuances of integration, such as with applications and databases, can also affect the business results of a cloud infrastructure choice. The challenge is to understand the unique business aspects of one's cloud infrastructure requirements. Then, it will be possible to select between AWS and Azure and achieve the desired business outcome" [15]. However, keep in mind that Azure vs. AWS price comparison is complicated by frequent price changes and new services. Modifications to existing services (e.g., latest-generation instances/VMs) also complicate comparisons because this tends to provide increased performance at the same price or sometime less. Similarly, the availability of a service, the region(s) in which the service is deployed, and the committed use or committed payment discount applied to the service can also make a difference [16]. In fact, Table 1-1 conveys on-demand pricing for Windows OS that includes the Type, vCPU, Memory, Azure, and AWS.

***Table 1-1.***  *On-Demand Pricing*

| TYPE | VCPU | MEM | AZURE | AWS |
| --- | --- | --- | --- | --- |
| General Purpose | 2 | 8GB | $0.6260 | $0.6680 |
| | 4 | 16GB | $0.8520 | $0.8560 |
| | 8 | 32GB | $1.7040 | $1.7120 |
| Compute Optimized | 2 | 4GB | $0.5780 | $0.6490 |
| | 4 | 8GB | $0.7980 | $0.8180 |
| | 8 | 16GB | $1.5960 | $1.6360 |
| Memory Optimized | 2 | 16GB | $0.6880 | $0.6850 |
| | 4 | 32GB | $0.9760 | $0.8900 |

Source: Compiled from CloudHealth Tech Staff (`www.cloudhealthtech.com/blog/azure-vs-aws-pricing`)

# Upgrade Recap

Although BallotOnline initially had concerns about upgrading their on-premises system, research helped BallotOnline improve their knowledge about integration of cloud computing architecture and the risk associated with utilizing cloud services. This also helped BallotOnline understand how to effectively conduct a risk analysis using a risk management matrix. This, too, helped BallotOnline understand risks associated with transitioning from an on-premises system to a cloud business system. BallotOnline also gained clarity about security for data at rest and risk measures for data at rest. The level of security implemented for data at rest determines the risk associated with that data. When data is at rest in the cloud, it can be secured by controlling access and implementing least privileges. This limits the number of personnel who can access the data. The same applies to data in transition and data in usage. Security approaches implemented to prevent unauthorized access to data typically include multi-factor log-in credentials that consist of a username and password. A thorough approach to defining a risk analysis is utilizing a risk factor table, which includes a date of the risk discovery, cause of the risk factor, type of risk management deployed, consequences of the risk discovered, full risk details, and risk owner or person(s) responsible for the risk exposure and exploitation, as well as the risk probability, that is, likely, unlikely, or very likely; the impact of the risk, that is, minor, moderately, or major; and the risk score, that is, acceptable risk medium or low and unacceptable risk high or extremely high. This also includes a response action type – that is, avoid, transfer, mitigate, or accept. Therefore, it is important to preplan the effective response actions deployed to mitigate the problem and methodologies needed to deter future risks.

When evaluating the risk associated with cloud computing architecture, safeguards must be considered, such as federal recommendations and guidelines. To effectively secure the cloud database, the US Department of Defense, the National Institute of Standards and Technology, and the Industry Standard Organization (ISO) have developed guidelines as precautionary tools of security, both for public and private sector enterprises, organizations, academia, and nonprofits. Furthermore, there are several relevant security issues encompassing cloud computing architecture, for instance, security concerns relating to risk areas – that is, external data storage, dependency on the "public" Internet, lack of control, multi-tenancy, and integration with internal security [17]. Compared with traditional technologies, the cloud has several unique features, for instance, scalability and resources belonging to cloud providers that are completely distributed, heterogeneous, and totally virtualized. When cloud service providers (CSPs) do not implement effective security management, the security of end users' data is left up to the service users. This makes your enterprise responsible for making sure access to the cloud and all of the data stored in the cloud is secured and protected effectively. Furthermore, because of the three cloud models, that is, Software as a Service (SaaS), Infrastructure as a Service (IaaS), and Platform as a Service (PaaS), it is important to understand what methods should be deployed to secure each service approach, once it is determined what cloud service provider best serves the needs of your enterprise.

# Summary

Making sure IT management and IT personnel responsible for overseeing the enterprise technology tools and systems are current with trends in AWS cloud services is essential. To achieve this goal, IT management and IT personnel should register to take part in ongoing AWS hybrid cloud training, offered at a low cost, if not free. IT management should be required to develop training material for all IT personnel to help them gain clarity on the new system and what their roles and responsibilities are in managing the security of data at rest. Training should include cybersecurity workplace training. The National Institute of Standards and Technology developed NIST SP 800-181 (see Notes) to encourage public and private sectors to establish awareness training defined by cybersecurity public policy developed by the organization. This policy delivers a clear understanding on the role cybersecurity workplace training plays in helping public and private sectors reduce threats of human error that create business liabilities. Conducting quarterly audits/assessments must become a norm and cover all security components that complete the on-premises system as well as the hybrid cloud. An audit should include all security policies implemented to assure IT personnel are knowledgeable of each security policy and are operating in compliance with each security policy. It is also important to have clarity on all components, including TCP connections, SDN and cloud deployment, declarative resource definitions, and AWS migration environment and configuration of web services. Doing so will help you increase your understanding of how essential cloud computing architecture management truly is. In the next chapter, you will gain vital information about cloud network engineering, another key component to understanding cloud services.

# Discussion Questions

1. What does total cost of ownership mean?

2. What is Amazon Aurora MySQL?

3. Why should your enterprise utilize an AWS TCO calculator?

4. Why are functional requirements essential?

5. What are the critical IT requirements relating to data storage?

6. What does the National Institute of Standards and Technology believe a cloud consumer needs to do with the adoption of a cloud-based solution?

7. Why is a risk management matrix important?

8. Who enacted guidelines as precautionary tools for cloud security?

9. What are the six components of the GDPR?

10. What state passed the Consumer Privacy Act and Privacy Right Act?

11. What are some of the physical security issues in the workplace?

12. What are two applicable laws dealing with intellectual property?

# CHAPTER 2

# Cloud Network Engineering

**Learning Objectives**

> Understand what Internet Protocol is.
>
> Comprehend what Transmission Control Protocol is.
>
> Understand what networking in the cloud means.
>
> Understand how to assess cloud Software as a Service for information system usage.

One of the most effective methods of sharing network engineering methods with executive members and stakeholders includes developing a technical report that provides essential details regarding your Internet Protocol, including packet switching, IP addressing, DNS, and IP routing. The report should also include information about IP subnetting, IP address classes, Classless Interdomain Routing (CIDR) notation, and subnets in a LAN. Furthermore, the report should provide information about Transmission Control Protocol, TCP connections, transport reliability, TCP sliding windows, software-defined networking, OpenFlow definition and purpose, networking in the cloud, cloud command line interface, declarative resource definition, and cloud Application Programming Interfaces (APIs). This chapter explains each of these components and shares information regarding how these components cemented BallotOnline's decision to partner with AWS for cloud services.

## Internet Protocol (IP)

"Internet Protocol is made up of a suite of communication protocols. The Transmission Control Protocol (TCP) and the Internet Protocol (IP) are two protocols to understand. The Internet Protocol suite not only includes lower-layer protocols (such as TCP and

© Bradley Fowler 2023
B. Fowler, *AWS for Public and Private Sectors*, https://doi.org/10.1007/978-1-4842-9048-4_2

IP), but specifies common applications such as electronic mail, terminal emulation, and file transfer" [1]. IP is a network layer protocol infused with address information and control information, which enables data packets to be routed across the Internet. IP is documented in RFC 791 and the key network layer protocol aligned with the Internet Protocol suite. IP has two roles: providing connectionless best-effort service of datagrams via internetwork and providing fragmentation and reassembly of datagrams to enable data links with various top-tier transmission unit sizes [2].

# Packet Switching

Packet switching is an invaluable component of Internet Protocol. After all, packet switching enables data to flow across the Internet. "With packet switching, messages are separated into small units called packets. Packets contain information about the sender and the receiver, the actual data being sent and information about how to reassemble the packets to reconstruct the original message. Packets travel along the network separately, based on their destination, network traffic, and other network conditions. When the packets reach their destination, they are reassembled in the proper order" [3]. Thus, when your enterprise utilizes its legacy system, all data transmitted via the Internet in an email, for instance, is provided a signature that includes the IP address assigned by the forwarding server.

# IP Addressing

IP addressing and the corresponding domain names utilized on behalf of your enterprise help identify computers that are immediately available via the Internet. IP addresses are numeric, such as 11.11.11.11, and are utilized by computers to exchange data. "IP addresses are allocated to each network to be used with the computers on that network, and there is a worldwide registration system for domain name registration" [4]. BallotOnline utilized several IP addresses that helped protect the transmission data, using subnetting and a virtual private network (VPN), which provided a layer of security to deter the IP address from being hacked and/or targeted by cybercriminals. Deploying several IP addresses helps protect the transmission and sharing of data. This adds an additional layer of security.

# DNS

The BallotOnline DNS (Domain Name System) enables the `www.ballotonline.com` web address to be readable by the server in an IP address format – that is, 11.11.11.11. When conducting research on the DNS to search for the IP address, Google provided clarity on a similar Domain Name System under the URL `www.ballot-online.com`. The data shared this information: `https://ballet-online.com.ipaddress.com` DNS "servers translate request for names into IP addresses, controlling which server an end user will reach when they type a domain name into their Web browser. Server translate requests are called queries" [5]. There are two types of DNS service: authoritative and recursive. Authoritative DNS "provides an update mechanism that developers use to manage their public DNS names, which answers DNS queries, translating domain names into IP addresses so computers can communicate with each other. Authoritative DNS has the final authority over a domain and is responsible for providing answers to recursive DNS servers with the IP address information" [6]. The recursive DNS role mirrors a hotel concierge; although it does not own any DNS records, it plays the role of an intermediary that attains the DNS information on behalf of your enterprise when it's requested. "If a recursive DNS has the DNS reference cached, or stored for a certain period, then it answers the DNS query by providing the source or IP information. If not, it passes the query to one or more authoritative DNS servers to find the information" [7].

# IP Subnetting

IP subnetting enables your enterprise to break the current IP address block into several small subnets. "Subnetting applies to IP addresses because this enables borrowing bits from the host portion of the IP address" [8]. In a sense, the IP address becomes three components: network, subnet, and host. To create a subnet for BallotOnline required collecting the last bit from the network component of the address – that is, 11 – and utilizing that to determine the number of subnets that needed to be created. For example, a Class C address normally has 24 bits for the network address and 8 for the host. However, you can borrow the leftmost bit of the host address and declare it as identifying the subnet. For instance, if the last bit is a 0, that will be one subnet; if the bit is a 1, it would be considered a second subnet. However, with only one borrowed bit, you can only have two possible subnets. On one hand, this will reduce the number of hosts your enterprise can have on the network to 127 (although 125 useable addresses are given, all zeros and all ones are not recommended addresses), down from 255. Keep in mind that utilizing a subnetting calculator can clarify how to effectively create IP subnets.

# IP Address Classes

IP address classes are a subcategory of IP subnetting. IP address classes range from A, B, C, D, and E. "Classes A, B, C offer addresses for networks of three distinct network sizes. Class D is only used for multicast, and class E reserved exclusively for experimental purposes" [9]. A Class A–type network envelopes the first 8 bits, that is, an octet, that identify the network, and the remaining 24 bits represent the host into that network. A Class B IP address, or binary address, starts with 10. This class decimal number can be between 128 and 191. However, "the number 127 is reserved for loopback, which is used for internal testing on the local machine" [10]. The first 16 bits or two octets identify the network. The remaining 16 bits explain the host encapsulating the network. A Class C IP address is utilized for small networks. Three octets are utilized to indent the network. IPs range between 192 and 223. The first two bits are set at 1, and the third bit is set at 0, making the first 24 bits of the addresses, and the remaining bits become host addresses. A local area network (LAN) relies on Class C IP addresses to enable connection with the network. Class D is not commonly utilized for regular networking protocol. It addresses the first three bits set at 1, and the fourth bit is set at 0. This class addresses the 32-bit network addresses. These values are identified multicast and grouped differently. Because there is no requirement to retrieve the host address from the IP address, Class D does not have a subnet mask. Class E is reserved and never defined, making this class often discardable.

# CIDR Notation

Classless Interdomain Routing "defines a notation methodology for network addressing that is used to specify the network portion of an IP address" [11]. Introduced in 1993 to extend the lifetime of IPv4, shockingly today, it is believed the industry is running out of available IP addresses. CIDR helps make it possible for your enterprise to fully utilize the public IPv4 address ranges assigned to the enterprise and open previously reserved address ranges. The RFC 1918 range enables CIDR to provide assignments of reserves, external non-routable networks, as mentioned with Class A, B, and C ranges. Such private networks can be utilized by your enterprise as an internal network. This will prevent every computer housed in your enterprise offices to have an assigned public IP address. This feature does provide a large portion of the solution for multiple issues that can arise. Utilizing private internal networks enables your enterprise to assign one or possibly several public IP addresses for connection to the external Internet while providing a wide scope of private address spaces for internal networks. "The design of CIDR notation with VLSM respects the old classful networking scheme while providing significantly more flexibility and IP address availability for private internal use by organizations of all sizes. Private address spaces as well as assigned public address spaces, can be easily split into subnets by adding bits to the netmask without consideration for network classes" [12].

# Subnets in a LAN

Because BallotOnline operates multiple branch offices in different regions and across geographical locations and availability zones, an AWS virtual local area network can be beneficial. Virtual LANs connect data paths between the on-premises network and service link VLAN and local gateway VLAN. The service link VLAN enables an exchange of data. The VLAN delivers access to an AWS region and enables the service linkage to connect and establish a reconnect to the region your enterprise selects. The service link also provides a VPN. This enables a secure connection. The local gateway VLAN enables VPN traffic from your enterprise VPN to the local LAN (local area network). Moreover, the VLAN helps AWS Instances effectively communicate with your on-premises network. This enables your enterprise to communicate with the Internet via its on-premises network.

An AWS VLAN was developed to separate service link and local gateway data paths in two isolated networks. Doing so enables your enterprise to elect which one of the enterprise networks to communicate with. This also enables your enterprise to isolate the service link from a local gateway network by utilizing multiple route tables on the enterprise local network device, commonly known as Virtual Routing and Forwarding Instances. Thus, it is recommended to enable your enterprise to manage all infrastructure deployed on its system. AWS explains clearly that outpost network devices require IP addresses on each VLAN to enable them to communicate with a local network device. Doing so establishes a Border Gateway Protocol (BGP) session. AWS recommends using a dedicated subnet with a /30 or /31 CIDR to demonstrate a logical point-to-point connection and recommends not bridging the VLANs between your local network devices.

# Subnetting Proposal

The subnetting proposal for BallotOnline enabled effective communication and data sharing across six branch offices. In fact, BallotOnline primarily elected to utilize a VLAN for all office branches. Doing so added additional layers of security to prevent packet sniffing during data transmission. Packet sniffing during transmission enables unauthorized users to access data and review content details. This often leads to data tampering and modification during transmission. To test if data has been tampered with during transmission, you can review the timestamp on the file and compare it with the timestamp the sender sent the data file. If there is a long time between sending and receiving, there is evidence of packet sniffing and/or tampering.

# TCP

TCP (Transmission Control Protocol) enables the transfer of data across the Internet. TCP is a component of IP, making it TCP/IP. This is how packet switching comes into play. "Support for TCP/IP is built into many operating systems, and IP addresses are commonly used in conjunction with other protocols, such as Ethernet to identify computers on a LAN" [13]. So, because your enterprise is operating multiple offices, internal TCP/IP transfer of data should be integrated through cloud computing. Doing so enables your enterprise to become more efficient. In fact, "today, DDoS mitigation, firewall, load balancing, and other important networking functions can all run in the cloud, eliminating the need for internal IT teams to build and maintain these services" [14]. As a result, it is recommended that your enterprise consider relying on a Network as a Service (NaaS). After all, NaaS provides flexibility, scalability, minimum maintenance, and cost savings and is bundled with security. Thus, I recommend researching to learn if NaaS is beneficial for your enterprise and its data sharing needs. Neglecting to do so can be costly and increase system security vulnerabilities.

# TCP Connections

When assessing TCP connections, it's clear "HTTP connections are nothing more than TCP connections, plus a few rules about how to use them. TCP connections are the reliable connections of the Internet" [15]. To send data accurately and quickly, your enterprise needs to know the basics of TCP. TCP enables HTTP (Hypertext Transfer

Protocol) to acquire a reliable bit pipe, which enables bytes to be stuffed on one side of a TCP connection and arrive correctly and in the correct order. In fact, TCP transmits data in small chunks classified as IP packets. This makes HTTP a top layer over TCP over IP. However, it is important to understand that using HTTP is considered unsecure. Therefore, it is recommended to deploy HTTPS; this enables cryptographic encryption layers to be applied – that is, SSL (Secure Sockets Layer), which adds an additional layer of security on each web page.

## Transport Reliability

TCP also ensures transfer reliability. In fact, the seven key components of TCP are connection orientation, point-to-point communication, total reliability, full-duplex communication, stream interface, reliable connection start-up, and graceful connection shutdown. However, TCP also embodies some issues that should be considered. First, unreliable communication messages can occur and cause messages to be lost, corrupted, and delayed. Be aware that TCP can cause the system to crash and reboot at any time. It can also create congestion, causing intermediate switches and routers to be overrun with data.

## TCP Sliding Windows

TCP sliding windows help determine the number of unacknowledged bytes that one system can transmit to another. "The sending system cannot send more bytes than space that is available in the received buffer on the receiving system. TCP on the sending system must wait to send more data until all bytes in the current send buffer are acknowledged by TCP on the receiving system" [16]. Thus, when your enterprise sends a message across the Internet, TCP sliding windows guarantee reliable delivery of the data. TCP will also assure your enterprise that its data was delivered in the correct order it was sent in as well as enforce flow control between the sender and the receiver.

## Software-Defined Networking

Software-defined networking divides data and control functions of networking devices, including routers, packet switches, and LAN switches, "with a well-defined Application Programming Interface between the two. In contrast, in most large enterprise networks, routers and other network devices encompass both data and control functions, making it difficult to adjust the network infrastructure and operation to large-scale addition of end systems, virtual machines, and virtual networks" [17]. Therefore, transitioning to cloud computing gives your enterprise the benefit of relying on software-defined networking and server virtualization. After all, server virtualization camouflages server resources, including the number and identity of each physical server, processor, and operating system, from server users. Furthermore, AWS deploys SDN within its cloud applications; this helps build private, public, and hybrid clouds that increase application deployment agility [18].

An AWS VLAN encompasses SDN, vSphere, and VMware Cloud. Furthermore, the AWS architecture is a custom design with network restrictions that enable increased performance and replication shared with regions and availability zones. This is an effective approach for the multiple regions and available zones your enterprise might occupy. Furthermore, utilizing AWS Outposts will decrease the need for continued in-house management. Additionally, AWS Outposts enables your enterprise to maintain some of its physical system at its primary headquarters as well as enable accessibility to other geographical locations, making the system accessible via the virtual network environment through a secure virtual private network (VPN) to protect data during transmission. This will enable your enterprise to reduce latency and data processing. Ideally, an AWS VLAN will enable your enterprise to select from fully integrated outpost configurations to design the use case(s) specifically for your business purposes.

# OpenFlow

OpenFlow is a popular standard of software-defined networking (SDN). "OpenFlow is a command-and-control protocol that includes communication over SSL/TLS protected channels, feature discovery and configuration of devices by the controller, and manages the forwarding tables on the switches. The OpenFlow protocol doesn't stipulate how the network is designed or managed" [19]. OpenFlow is designed in the OpenFlow Switch Specification that is published by the Open Networking Foundation (ONF). ONF is a consortium of software providers, content delivery networks, and networking equipment vendors; their purpose is to promote software-defined networking [20].

# SDN Enables Cloud Deployment

SDN is integrated in AWS Outposts. This integration increases security and encryption on all data at rest and in transmission. AWS provides your enterprise the ability to increase layers of security on data at rest. Doing so provides scalable and efficient encryption that includes flexible key management options, such as AWS Key Management Service that enables your enterprise to elect AWS to manage the encryption keys. Because AWS delivers committed hardware-integrated cryptographic key storage encapsulated in AWS CloudHSM, this enables, your enterprise to satisfy its compliance requirements. Furthermore, AWS delivers encrypted message queues for the delivery of sensitive data utilizing Service-Side Encryption (SSE) designed for Amazon SQS. When there are Connected Status problems, it is recommended to verify connectivity to the AWS region from within your enterprise network. Of course, AWS renders the support needed if problems consistently exist.

# Networking in the Cloud

Networking in the cloud increases security and decreases potential risk associated with the transmission of data across the Internet. To help achieve this goal, networking in the cloud aligns with a VPC (virtual private cloud), which encompasses subnets to increase privacy and security. Virtual Internet traffic transmitted via a network within a VPC is managed by route tables that define protocol delegating how VPC subnets communicate. Each subnet within the VPC is associated with a route table, and a public subnet is required to help a route table connect to an Internet gateway. Networking in the cloud encompasses some components of IT infrastructure that enables your enterprise to host its network capabilities and resources in a public or private cloud managed by your enterprise in-house IT team or by your third-party external source – that is, Amazon Web Services. Thus, your enterprise can either utilize on-premises cloud networking resources to establish a private cloud network. Or your enterprise can utilize cloud-based network resources in a public cloud or a hybrid cloud infrastructure. Doing so enables your enterprise to rely on network resources, such as virtual routers, firewalls, and bandwidth and network management software in concert with additional tools and functions as the enterprise needs.

Networking in the cloud increases agility, delivers differentiation, increases time to market, and optimizes scalability. After all, networking in the cloud has become a standardized model to enable building and delivering applications to support business endeavors. Networking in the cloud plays a critical role in enabling your enterprise to address its expansion, including regional and redundancy planning. Thus, adopting networking in the cloud positions your enterprise among the top Fortune 500 corporations who are leveraging multiple cloud infrastructures while relying on various cloud service providers to achieve their goals.

An AWS VPC and associated networking components are rated top of the line and come with a service agreement guarantee. AWS has built its reputation rooted in defining cloud infrastructure that adapts to the needs of any business and delivers a dynamic customer service support team that works closely with in-house IT teams. An AWS VPC is an isolated virtual network associated with a customer's private account. This limits who has access to the data hosted in the cloud environment provided by AWS.

In fact, a VPC will create a virtual network that will be dedicated to your enterprise's AWS account. This account will be isolated from other virtual networks within the AWS cloud. Within this framework is Amazon EC2 Instance. This enables your enterprise to specify an IP address range for the virtual private cloud, increase subnets, associate security groups, as well as configure route tables. A subnet is a range of IP addresses that would include your enterprise VPC. Your enterprise can launch AWS resources into a specified subnet while using a public subnet resource that is connected to the Internet and a private subnet for resources that won't be connected to the Internet [21]. However, to effectively protect the Amazon Web Services resources in each designated subnet, your enterprise needs to establish multiple layers of security that include a security group and network access control lists (ACLs).

In fact, the associated networking components delivered with the AWS VPC include Internet gateways, carrier gateways, NAT devices for your enterprise VPC, DNS support, and a prefix list. The Internet gateway is a horizontally scaled, redundant VPC infrastructure that enables communication between your enterprise VPC and the Internet. Utilizing this component enables your enterprise to perform network address translation for Instances that your enterprise IT team assigns a public IPv4 address to. After all, the Internet gateway supports IPv4 and IPv6 traffic. However, Internet gateways will not cause availability risks or bandwidth constraints on your enterprise network traffic. Furthermore, please keep in mind there is no additional cost for having an Internet gateway associated with your enterprise account. So there would not be additional cost if your enterprise has an Internet gateway associated with your AWS account.

Carrier gateways have two distinct purposes: to allow inbound traffic from a carrier network in specific locations and to allow outbound traffic to the carrier network and the Internet. A carrier gateway renders support for IPv4 traffic. NAT devices for your enterprise VPC enable Instances in private subnets to be connected to the Internet, additional VPCs, and on-premises networks. Such Instances can communicate with services outside the VPC, but cannot receive connections that were not requested by your enterprise. NAT devices replace IPv4 addresses of an Instance with addresses of the NAT device. So, when sending response traffic to an Instance, the NAT device will translate the addresses back to your enterprise original source IPv4 addresses. Your enterprise can then utilize managed NAT devices that AWS offers, such as a NAT gateway. Or your enterprise can design its own NAT device using an EC2 Instance, which is called a NAT Instance.

With DNS support for your enterprise VPC, your enterprise can utilize a public or private IPv4 address to communicate within the network of the Instance, using either an EC2 or a VPC. "Domain Name System (DNS) is a standard by which names used on the Internet are resolved to their corresponding IP addresses" [22]. DNS also helps resolve DNS hostnames to their correlating IP addresses. So either Amazon delivers a DNS server with your enterprise VPC. Or your enterprise can use its own DNS server and create a new set of DHCP options for its VPC.

Lastly, AWS provides a prefix list, which is a set of one or more CIDR blocks. Your enterprise can utilize prefix list blocks to configure and manage its security groups and route tables. Your enterprise can also create a prefix list from its IP addresses that it frequently utilizes and reference that list as a set in the security group rules and routes, instead of referencing them by themselves. Prefix lists are delivered in two ways: as customer-managed prefix lists or AWS-managed prefix lists. Furthermore, taking advantage of an AWS VPC in regions and availability zones to secure and assure availability of infrastructure will help keep cost low and reduce security risk tremendously. Because your enterprise may have several offices in several locations, it is best to establish multiple VPCs that enable Internet connectivity with little security risks. Doing so will help eliminate exposure of sensitive data and reduce potential vulnerabilities that may not be identifiable by the IT team immediately. Taking precautions to secure each office across various regions and zones is planning an effective mitigation strategy to protect the enterprise from unauthorized intrusion and hackers.

# Cloud Command Line Interface

Utilizing Amazon Web Services (AWS) cloud command line interface enables your enterprise to create, monitor, update, and delete stacks from your enterprise system's terminal. BallotOnline utilized AWS CLI to automate actions through scripts. After all, AWS CLI is considered an open source tool that helped BallotOnline interact with AWS services through commands that BallotOnline deployed using its command line shell. Utilizing this tool enables your enterprise to begin running commands that deploy functionality equivalent to those provided by the browser-based Amazon Web Services Management Console, from the command dashboard in your enterprise terminal program.

Cloud CLI enables your enterprise to directly access the public APIs of Amazon Web Services as well as explore service capability within AWS CLI. Furthermore, your enterprise will be able to develop shell scripts to effectively manage its resources. More importantly, your enterprise's reliance on AWS enables customizations for your enterprise AWS CLI. Customizations include higher-level commands, which simplify utilizing a service with a complex API [23]. The advantage of utilizing AWS CLI includes your enterprise being able to utilize its own commands to work effectively and efficiently every time a command is deployed. Using CLI also enables your enterprise to deploy repetitive tasks without stress. After all, CLI needs less memory to utilize compared with other interfaces [24]. Of course, BallotOnline's usage of AWS CLI in provisioning, management enabled increased scalability and usage of keypairs. Keypair usage with EC2 AWS CLI enables connectivity to AWS EC2 Instances. To achieve this goal, your enterprise needs to provide the keypair created by the IT team to Amazon EC2 when creating an Instance as well as to continue utilizing that same keypair to authenticate each time someone from the enterprise connects to the enterprise Instance. Creating a keypair with AWS CLI requires using the command line "aws ec2 create-key-pair" with the - query option as well as the - output txt option to effectively pipe your enterprise private key directly into a file. However, please keep in mind that your enterprise private key is not stored in AWS servers and can be retrieved "only" when the keypair is created. Furthermore, if lost, your enterprise cannot recover the keypair at a later time or date. Instead, your enterprise will need to create a new keypair. In fact, your enterprise can display and delete its keypairs. Of course, AWS provides references to help your enterprise gain clarity regarding these concerns. Thus, please keep in mind to always consult AWS regarding concerns and questions concerning keypair development, usage, storage, and accessibility.

# Declarative Resource Definitions

One method of executing a scripting command is describing what type of effect is desired for the execution command deployed. Using declarative programming, your enterprise decides what it wants to achieve, not how it wants to achieve it, and the AWS IaC (Infrastructure as Code) framework configures the steps to deploy to meet the command goals. For instance, when BallotOnline provided a description of desired configuration through a designed template using declarative notations, commonly it relied on YAML (YAML Ain't Markup Language) or JSON (JavaScript Object Notation).

The advantage of using declarative resource definitions within AWS CLI is that your enterprise can rely on AWS CloudFormation (CF) to manage the deployment of a command line input without much concern if AWS is going to deliver the outcome requested. Many declarative coding approaches embody an imperative element, and CloudFormation configuration language is no exception [25]. Moreover, your enterprise will be able to declare common resources deployed across various stacks into one template snippet and reference that snippet in other templates your enterprise may create later. Your enterprise can also easily manage and maintain this common code in one safe and secure place and reuse the configuration when your enterprise needs to. Furthermore, the AWS CloudFormation (CF) framework utilizes declarative templates to determine configurations of cloud resources called stacks. The CloudFormation designing tools enable your enterprise to create and configure using a GUI-based tool. That tool creates a template skeleton. Once the design is done, AWS CloudFormation enables your enterprise to provision stacks automatically.

# Cloud APIs

A cloud Application Programming Interface is another SaaS (Software as a Service) Amazon Web Services (AWS) provides customers. Utilizing this API enables your enterprise to easily develop, implement, and manage your enterprise's entire cloud Infrastructure as Code (IaC) with the use of Instances and gateways, enveloped in AWS EC2 and network and development dashboards. Relying on AWS cloud APIs makes it easy and simple to manage what happens with your enterprise cloud infrastructure. After all, API Gateway manages all tasks required to accept and process up to hundreds of thousands of concurrent API calls, including traffic management, authorization and access control, monitoring, and API version management. Furthermore, API Gateway offers a serverless developer portal that enables API publishers to effectively connect with API subscribers as well as monitor, manage, and update APIs [26].

There are many benefits that your enterprise can gain utilizing this approach. First, AWS API Gateway enables your enterprise to utilize Signature Version 4 authentication, which enables your enterprise to use Identity and Access Management as well as access policies to authorize who can access your enterprise APIs and additional resources your enterprise relies on through the AWS customer account. Additionally, this medium of SaaS manages all flow of traffic your enterprise's API receives. This enables your enterprise some freedom to focus on business logic and services, instead of maintaining infrastructure. This also gives your enterprise access to a dashboard to visually monitor calls to the business. After all, the AWS API Gateway console is integrated with Amazon CloudWatch, which provides a full visibility into the back-end performance metrics, that is, API calls, latency, and error rates.

AWS delivers clarity with its API services, so much so your enterprise is able to create and design using web applications that easily interact with other components your enterprise chooses within its AWS EC2 applications. Your enterprise is also able to utilize two different APIs – that is, Restful APIs and WebSocket APIs. With Restful APIs, your enterprise can rely on API proxy functionality and management features, like usage plans and APIs keys. Your enterprise also is able to rely on WebSocket APIs as a stateful front end for an AWS service (such as Lambda or DynamoDB) or for an HTTP endpoint. The WebSocket API invokes your enterprise back end based on the content of the messages received from a client's app, much different than Restful API, which receives and responds to inquiries. WebSocket API helps two-way communication that occurs between client apps and your enterprise back end. This means the back end can forward callback messages to any connected client your enterprise may be working with.

Furthermore, your enterprise could also utilize cloud APIs, such as Python SDK (Software Development Kit), to develop, provision, and manage its cloud environment. After all, AWS cloud APIs using Python SDK are just as easy to understand, develop, deploy, and manage, with little knowledge of coding in Python. Using a Boto3 command line, BallotOnline was able to integrate the Python application, library, or script with its AWS CloudFormation and EC2 environment. "Boto3 has two distinct levels of APIs. Client (or 'low-level') APIs that provide one-to-one mappings to the underlying HTTP API operations" [27]. Of course, understanding this is helpful in determining if the partnership with AWS is worth it or not. After all, with the support rendered by AWS, your enterprise will be ready to begin its migration from the old legacy on-premises system to full cloud infrastructure. However, to effectively achieve this, it is important to understand the AWS migration and configuration of web services.

# AWS Migration Environment and Configuration of Web Services

Developing the AWS migration environment requires reliance on virtual servers or virtual machines hosted within EC2 Instances provided by AWS. Virtual environments are defined by software separating the physical infrastructure to enable several resources to be transmitted simultaneously. Virtual machines and virtual machine software enable several operating systems and applications to transmit in alignment with several hardware devices simultaneously. The benefits of virtualization are efficiency, an ability to utilize several resources, and flexibility. Virtualized environments provide applications, networking, and storage and engulf different categories of virtualization in concert with traditional hardware and operating systems.

Virtualized systems enable computers to efficiently mirror other systems and different hardware-defined devices, that is, computers and mobile devices. Virtualized servers and hypervisor software enable the ability to mirror virtual machines on a host server. This enables each virtual server to navigate its individual operating system. Furthermore, the hypervisor enables the ability to operate above the host's operating system and substitute it. Virtualization is a pillar of cloud computing, particularly within the private cloud architecture. For instance, this approach enables a divide of a single hardware system into several effective components of that system. In fact, virtualization is a key asset to developing, implementing, and managing cloud-based architecture. Not only is there flexibility but there is an increase of security because multi-authentication is deployed to limit who has access to the cloud infrastructure and information assets.

However, keep in mind that there are three components within migration to cloud that should be assessed: servers, network, and storage. Legecy system servers are bulky physical objects that require space, and there's a particular climate to host these bulky objects because of the increase volume of electricity required to operate them as well as physical security to limit accessibility. This commonly includes the use of CCTV installations and biometric security to safeguard access to the area where physical servers exist. With virtual servers, the need for increased security is enveloped in hosting services of the virtual private cloud, that is, Amazon Web Services. Utilizing a simple keypair system that can be deployed within the AWS EC2 system dashboard helps reduce the threat of security risk and limits who has access to such vital information.

Networks in a physical environment also pose risk. There is a decrease in the security of these technology assets, while there is an increase of accessibility because of the on-site existence of these technology tools. Virtual networks hosted within the AWS EC2 dashboard become almost nonexistent and incapable of being tampered. With cloud networking, a virtual local area network is programmable, making it easier to manage and secure. Cloud networks also make communication with external computer systems less vulnerable. After all, security groups play an important role within cloud networks and are easy to define within the AWS EC2 dashboard. This is beneficial because it helps establish access control and rules, which your enterprise can define in alignment with its regulations and policy.

Most important, storage within a physical environment embodies concerns of security and file tampering. With a physical storage environment, there is increase concern enveloping who has access to physical storage. Aligning storge needs with policy within the enterprise and limiting who has access to valuable information assets decreases the risk and deploys a risk management strategy that helps define a storage system that is impenetrable. Thus, relying on AWS cloud infrastructure storage capability decreases concerns of risk management and enables your enterprise to assure both customers and the government that effective security methodologies are taken seriously and implemented to safeguard the information collected, to help deter information asset tampering. Therefore, utilizing AWS cloud storage increases value of any proposed environment migration.

Another important asset is AWS content delivery network, which can be utilized in concert with object storage. For instance, with direct attached storage within the current legacy system, access time is not always expedient. Furthermore, this storage capability is designed for short-term and temporary usage. When paired with virtual instance storage, data is lost if the Instances are stopped. This impacts the ability for stored data to be successfully backed up as needed. There are also two additional network storage capabilities: network attached storage and storage area network. Network attached storage attaches to a computer from other computers that access data files and folders across the network, while storage area network enables computers to consider the partition like DAS devices. Using the cloud environment storage capability is an innovative approach to secure data and reduce cost.

Keep in mind that it is invaluable to learn how to add a security rule to enable HTTP connection to your enterprise-proposed Instances. In fact, this will help provide in-depth clarity on how to effectively deploy auto-scaling groups and load balancers. Both components help define a secure cloud infrastructure that enables your enterprise to upgrade from its current legacy system with minimum stress and concern of potential security vulnerabilities occurring in the immediate and far-reaching future. Cloud services within business environments are a beneficial asset that continue to gain global recognition for their flexibility and scalability. However, cloud environments also are useful for enabling improved communication and data sharing. In fact, research conveys that "with cloud computing, employees can work from anywhere at any time, which improves efficiency and produces better-quality work" [28]. Working with Amazon Web Services for cloud infrastructure for your enterprise web services not only increases innovation of services by controlling potential risk associated with information assets but reduces the threat and vulnerabilities encompassed in utilizing cloud environment web services. After all, AWS encapsulates clients' services with a Service Level Agreement and has partnered with the federal government who enacted the Federal Risk and Authorization Management Program. This assures that cloud service providers align their policy and services with the National Institute of Standards of Technology Special Publication 800 series, to deploy effective accountability to assure consumers services acquired through AWS are effective, efficient, and reliable with little security concerns. This increases the feasibility of partnering with Amazon Web Services for the cloud infrastructure for your enterprise and its web service needs.

Keep in mind that services established with AWS operating within the US East and West Regions have been granted Joint Authorization Provisional Authority to operate and moderate impact levels. This enables effective baseline security to be infused within AWS services in alignment with the compliance program. This, too, reduces concerns about potential risk enveloped in the services rendered by Amazon Web Services. Most importantly, feasibility is engulfed in operating within the perimeters of the CIA triad, that is, confidentiality, integrity, and availability. When services are rendered in alignment with these standards, there is an increased assurance that quality control is deployed and a level of increased professionalism is achieved with every effort to assure your enterprise receives efficient and quality service. Thus, working with this service provider is a benefit toward maintaining control over the storage of sensitive data. After all, AWS thrives to provide a cloud infrastructure that can be modified to meet the needs of any enterprise, with T-shirt size scalability – that is, small, medium, large, or extra-large. Working with this enterprise certainly will be a partnership worth fostering.

# Summary

AWS renders a secure opportunity to effectively back up systems and deploy recovery plans. However, you must effectively develop, implement, and manage disaster recovery plans for cloud infrastructure to align with standards established under the NIST SP 800-144 Guidelines on Security and Privacy in Public Cloud Computing and NIST SP 500-291 Cloud Computing Standards Roadmap (see Notes). It is also important to understand that business continuity planning plays a key role in helping your enterprise stay ahead of the competition. Having knowledge of what is important helps your enterprise achieve its goals and objectives with little downtime and minimum risk. In the next chapter, you will gain information regarding cloud premigration considerations, cloud migration tool assessments, and AWS Application Discovery Service. You will also acquire details regarding agent-based options and agentless options as well as learn about the value of evaluation of discovery application and infrastructure data and migration recommendations. Attaining this information will help you effectively decide to partner with Amazon Web Services (AWS) for your business cloud system.

# Discussion Questions

1. What is Internet Protocol?

2. What is packet switching?

3. What does IP addressing provide?

4. What are the two types of Domain Name Service?

5. What is authoritative DNS?

6. What is recursive DNS?

7. What will IP subnetting provide your enterprise?

8. What can an IP subnetting calculator provide?

9. What does CIDR notation help your enterprise with?

10. What service does AWS offer to separate service links?

11. What can a subnetting proposal offer your enterprise?

12. What does Transfer Control Protocol provide?

13. What do TCP sliding windows provide?

14. What does software-defined networking do?

15. What is OpenFlow capable of providing?

# CHAPTER 3

# Infrastructure Planning and Migration

**Learning Objectives**

Understand the significance of infrastructure planning.

Understand migration prerequisites.

Understand how to effectively assess migration tools.

Understand AWS Application Discovery Service.

Infrastructure planning is a vital method to preparing the dynamics of your enterprise's information system. The sensitive data created and shared globally by your enterprise's technology framework is developed and transmitted across the Internet. Therefore, an enterprise infrastructure plan is mandatory! Infrastructure planning increases compliance awareness and security and promotes budget management. Thus, comprehending the key methods to secure the information developed, stored, and shared across the Internet in the cloud requires a strategic security model. This chapter will help you understand cloud premigration considerations, cloud migration tool assessments, AWS Application Discovery Service, agent-based options, agentless options, cloud migration prerequisites, cloud migration tool sets, AWS Database Migration Service, data migration of MySQL databases to AWS, cloud monitoring and management options, and the benefits of AWS Trusted Advisor. Additionally, you will learn about cut-out/rollback options and gain post-migration recommendations to improve your knowledge of AWS and the infrastructure planning and migration model deployed on behalf of BallotOnline.

Cloud infrastructure planning for BallotOnline required assessing the following technical factors: complexity, security architecture, and network support services. However, to effectively understand these technical factors requires understanding

© Bradley Fowler 2023
B. Fowler, *AWS for Public and Private Sectors*, https://doi.org/10.1007/978-1-4842-9048-4_3

the Software Development Life Cycle, which helps define your approach to your enterprise's cloud migration. Relying on the Software Development Life Cycle requires understanding the five-step process, including conducting a feasibility analysis that helps you conduct migration planning, migration execution, testing and migration validation, as well as monitoring and maintenance. The feasibility analysis phase is helpful in determining if a cloud migration will be financially and technically feasible for the enterprise. The second phase focuses on the assessment of existing IT environments. But because attention was focused on BallotOnline cloud service needs for their email, software development, and backup and archiving, it was essential to gain knowledge about each application that supports migration as well as the services AWS delivers to help with migration. Thus, migration execution is the next phase; this phase requires you to assess all of the current information systems being considered for migration. This includes understanding data extraction, code modification, architecture recovery, and the actual cloud migration. Additionally, testing and migration validation is required. This enables you to test and evaluate the system to assure it operates as needed. The final phase is maintaining and monitoring the newly migrated system. In fact, the following steps are required to achieve this goal:

- Clearly understand what is expected for the cloud information system.

- Know your role and responsibilities as the cloud architect for your enterprise.

- Consider conducting a deep-cloud migration with reliance on AWS S3.

- Determine if your enterprise will utilize a single or multiple cloud service providers.

- Create cloud KPIs.

- Determine performance baselines.

- Assess each migration component, that is, email, software development, and backup and archiving.

- Conduct essential refactoring as needed or switch production as required.

- Review the application resource allocation.

# Cloud Premigration Considerations

Determining your enterprise's business acumen, the needs and objectives for upgrading to the cloud, and what type of cloud will best serve the needs of your enterprise is challenging. The assessment conducted for the BallotOnline information system enabled me to determine the best strategy and services required to meet the needs of this entity. Utilizing Infrastructure as a Service (IaaS) was the final assessment because this approach enables an enterprise to achieve its goal of migrating to the cloud. In fact, to successfully achieve this goal for your enterprise, you will need to evaluate the scope of applications AWS offers to meet your enterprise individual needs. One important component to utilize is the AWS Simple Monthly Calculator to predetermine the estimated cost for monthly usage fees. You can access this calculator at the following link: `https://calculator.s3.amazonaws.com/index.html`.

Furthermore, you will need to utilize the AWS Total cost of ownership calculator to refine business use case. Doing so creates transparency in pricing, assesses the service cost for various components needed to effectively operate in the cloud, as well as estimates exports. Next, you will need to assess if the cloud will work as a landing zone for each application in scope as well as create security policies and determine what type of policy level should be considered for each tier of the enterprise's hierarchy. For instance, the AWS Policy Generator enables AWS account owners/administrators to determine the number of characters to utilize for a password and the type of characters, that is, letters, symbols, alphanumericals, and upper- and lowercase, as well as the type of authentication factors to implement for additional layers of security. Thus, you will need to create keypairs, establish user groups or user accessibilities, and test these environments to make sure they are operating correctly and effectively.

Additionally important is electing the correct geographical regions and setting the time zones for your enterprise as well as establishing permissions. Since BallotOnline was utilizing a MySQL server, it was important to determine whether to stay on MySQL or determine a method to move off this system. After all, AWS shares three common strategies for migrating a SQL Server database to AWS: rehost, re-platform, and re-architect (refactor) [1]. Since BallotOnline decided to utilize AWS EC2 Instance, rehost was their best option. Rehost does not require modification of the current SQL database, nor does it require changing the operating system from Linux or Windows. In fact, no changes are required for the database software; neither is there a need for configuration. However, you must determine the following issues:

- Resiliency for both computer and networking

- Log analysis and metric collection

- Effective management of user experiences

- Determining software compatibilities

# Cloud Migration Tool Assessment

AWS Database Migration Service and NetApp OnCommand Insight are two migration tools. To help you understand the benefits of each migration tool, Figure 3-1 provides a comparison reporting the advantages of both tools.

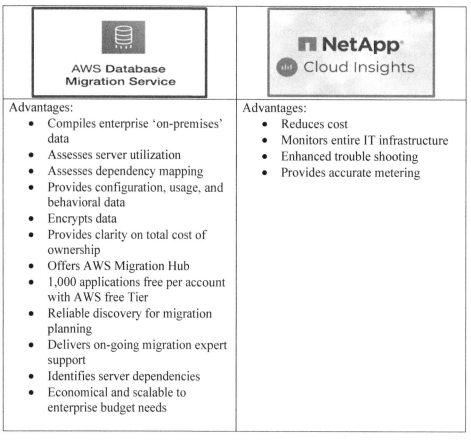

**Figure 3-1.** *Comparison report*

AWS Database Migration Service embodies increased value that enables an enterprise to accomplish its short- and long-term goals and objectives, such as managing an effective and secure cloud environment with the use of the enterprise current on-premises datacenter. AWS services outrank NetApp OnCommand Insight because AWS delivers scalability that is economical and flexible. In addition, AWS has a service support team 24/7/365, willing to support your enterprise regarding questions about migration, cloud usage, and security. AWS is easy to partner with to deploy a successful enterprise migration. In fact, Figure 3-2 provides details and descriptions of what is required when creating an EC2 Instance.

First, you will need to elect the Amazon Linux 2 machine image for a 64-bit device or 32-bit device and select the Instance type, that is, t2micro. This is a free tier, which has a limit on the amount of data that can be utilized. You will need to assess each level of Instances to determine how much usage your enterprise will incur. Doing so will save time and frustration as you work with EC2 Instances throughout the system life cycle.

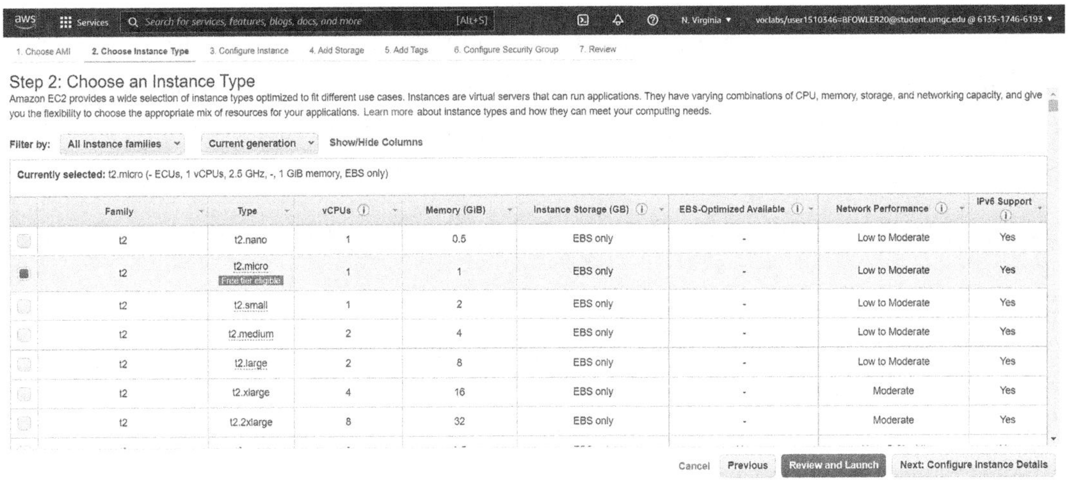

***Figure 3-2.*** *Instance type selections*

Next, you will need to configure the Instance details by electing the number of Instances desired, the network, and the subnet, as well as selecting a DNS hostname, that is, enabling resource-based IPv4. Then, you will need to establish a new IAM role, that is, Lab Instance Profile, and elect to configure protection against accidental termination. You also can enable CloudWatch detailed monitoring and increase storage. As you experience the Configuration Instance Details, you should review the dashboard to gain clarity on additional components listed that can increase your enterprise usage and security. Figure 3-3 shows details of configuring the Instance details.

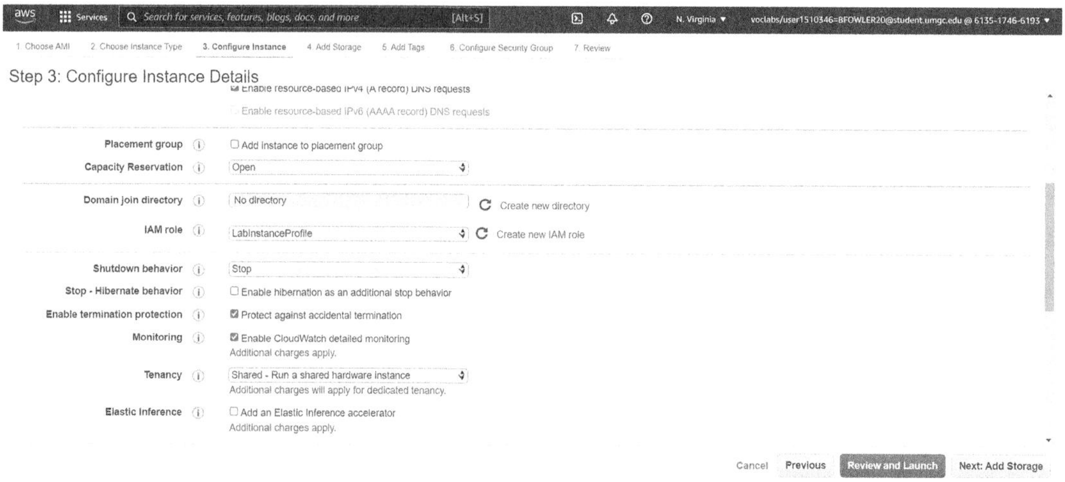

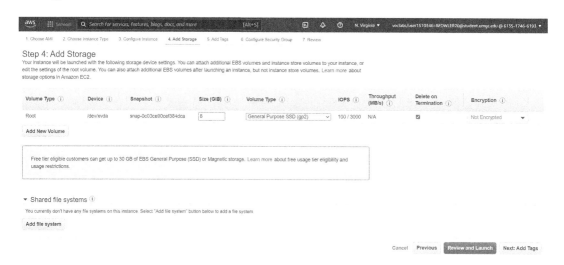

*Figure 3-3.* Configuring Instance details

Keep in mind, when adding storage, the default Volume Type is set as Root. Your Size (GIB) will differ greatly than what was set for BallotOnline. Figure 3-4 shows the Size (GIB) was set to 8 for BallotOnline and the Volume Type was set as General Purpose SSD (gp2).

*Figure 3-4.* Adding storage

Next, you will want to add tags, which includes selecting case-sensitive key and value. The Key was classified BallotOnline; Figure 3-5 provides a visual of this screen selection.

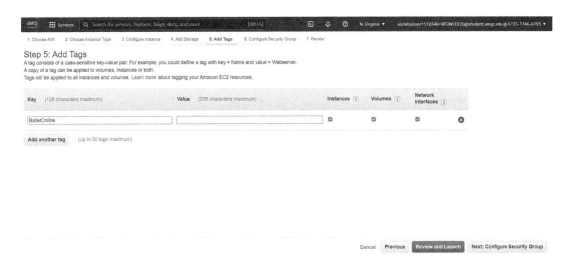

***Figure 3-5.*** *Adding tags*

Next, you will need to configure the security group name and select the type of security group – SSH. You will also establish the Protocol as TCP and set the Port Range to 22. Then, you will designate the Custom Source, that is, BallotOnline, prior to the Review and Launch. Figure 3-6 provides an example image of the system frame.

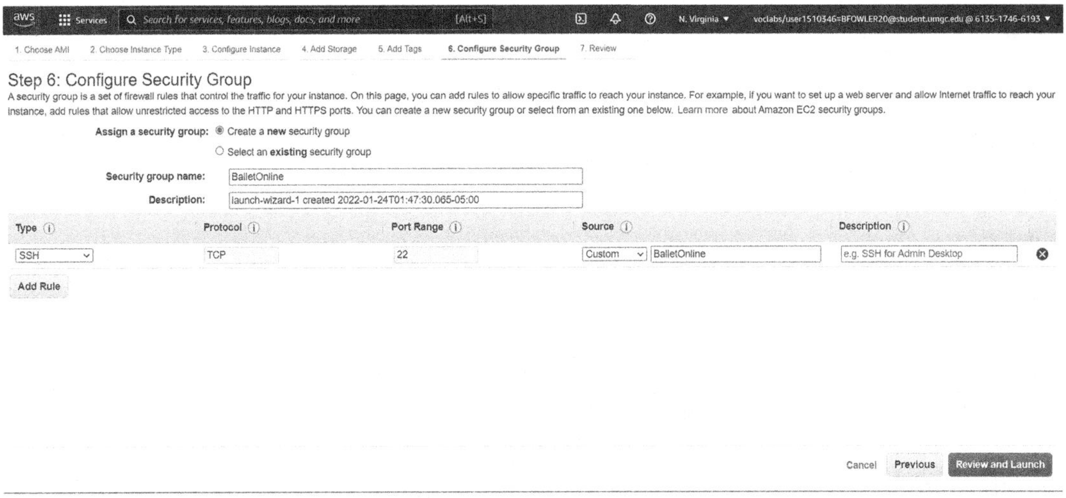

***Figure 3-6.*** *Configuration of a security group*

Then, you must elect the Source, which requires an IP address that is inaccessible to public users. Figure 3-7 provides an example.

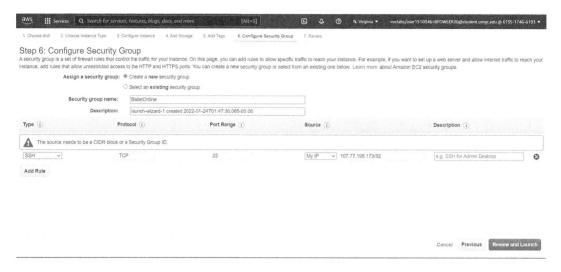

***Figure 3-7.***

Then, you will review the Instance launch. Figure 3-8 shares an example.

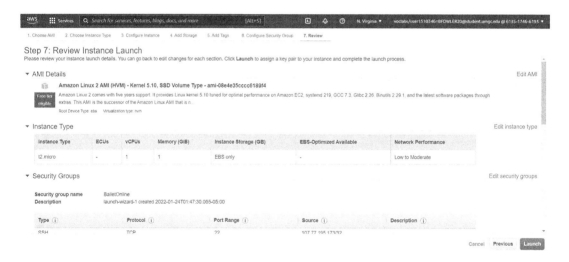

***Figure 3-8.*** *Review of the Instance launch*

Afterward, you will create a keypair to limit the authorization access to only an administrator with administrator privileges, that is, your enterprise name. The type of keypair assigned should be RSA, and the keypair must be downloaded and saved in a secure file for quick accessibility as needed. Figure 3-9 provides an example.

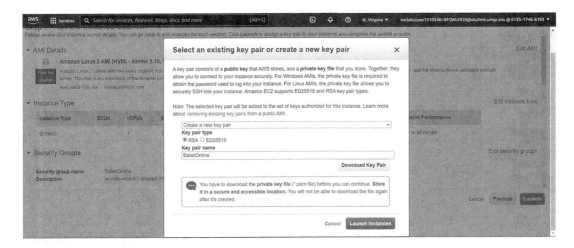

***Figure 3-9.*** *Keypair selection and creation*

Next, you will have access to the Instance launch status. Figure 3-10 provides an example.

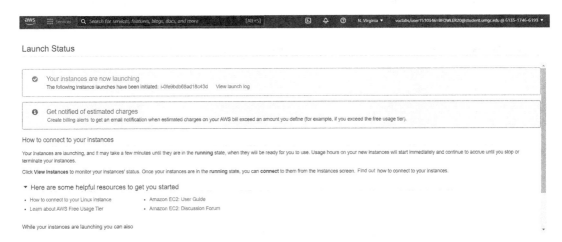

***Figure 3-10.*** *Proof of Instance launch*

Figure 3-11 provides an example of an active Instance.

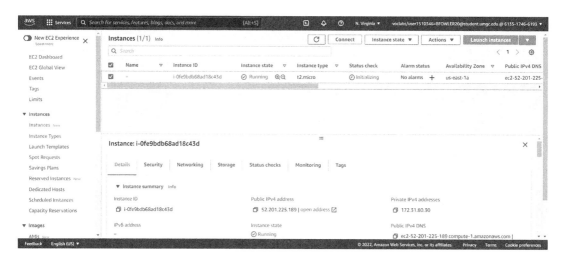

***Figure 3-11.*** *Successful running Instance*

Next, you will create a LAMP stack, which enables you to compile four pieces of server-side software commonly utilized as the foundation for developing websites. Figures 3-12 and 3-13 share an example of the Create stack dashboard.

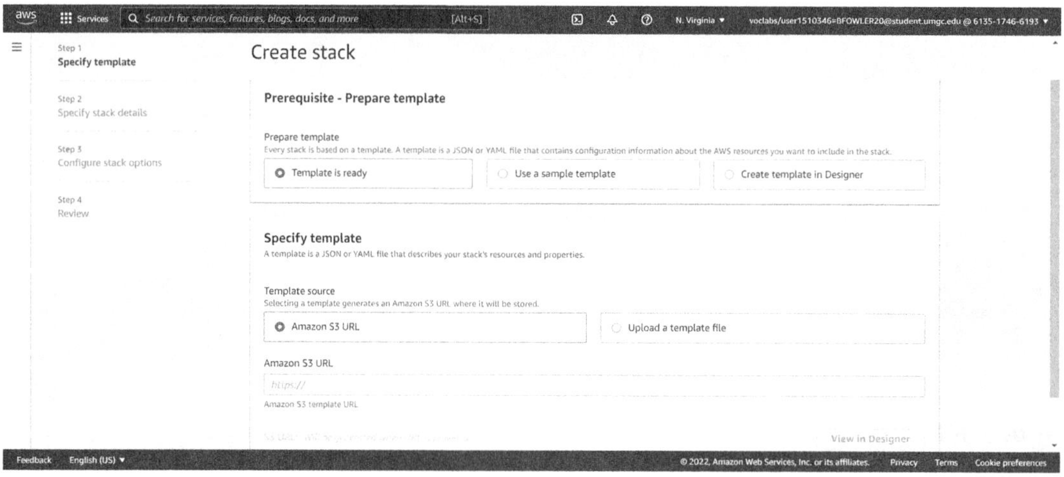

***Figure 3-12.*** *Stack creation*

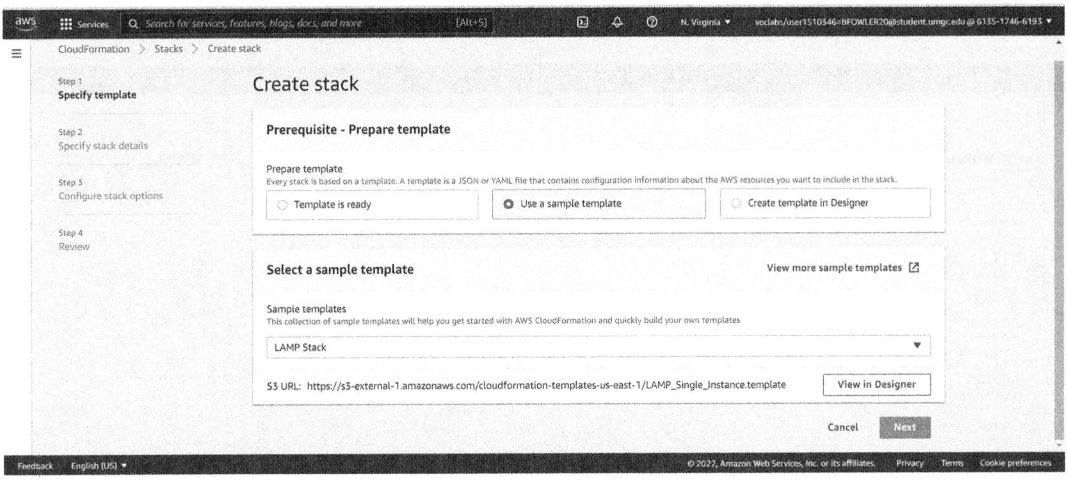

***Figure 3-13.*** *Selecting a stack template*

Of course, you must specify the stack details, including the name, DBName, DBPassword, and DBUser, as well as create the Instance type and set it as Default. Figure 3-14 provides an example of the specified stack details.

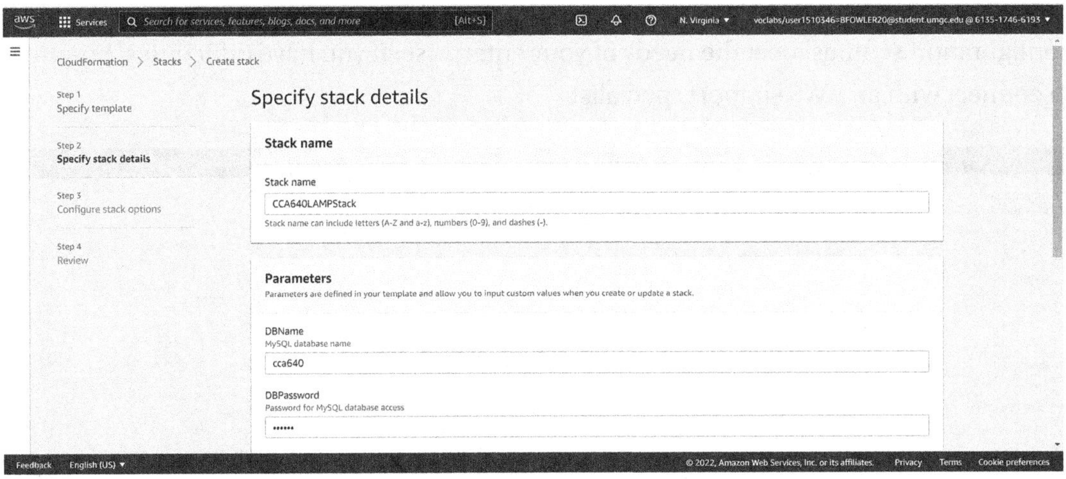

***Figure 3-14.*** *Selecting the stack details*

Figure 3-15 shows that BallotOnline LAMPStack was created.

***Figure 3-15.*** *Successful LAMPStack created*

Then, you will need to establish an IAM user, which requires you to specify a template. Figure 3-16 shows the IAM dashboard. Configurations will differ from enterprise to enterprise, so be sure to research the dashboard and determine what configuration settings meet the needs of your enterprise. If you have difficulties, be sure to connect with an AWS support specialist.

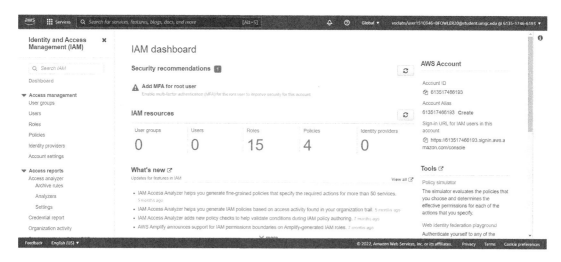

***Figure 3-16.*** *IAM dashboard evaluation*

You may receive an alert message denying access to configure the downloaded file. Relax and review the message. If you do not have clarity on what is needed to proceed, please be sure to contact AWS support services, which will guide you through each step. Figure 3-17 provides an example of pop-ups that can occur on your screen during development. Take time to review screen messages; doing so will decrease your frustration.

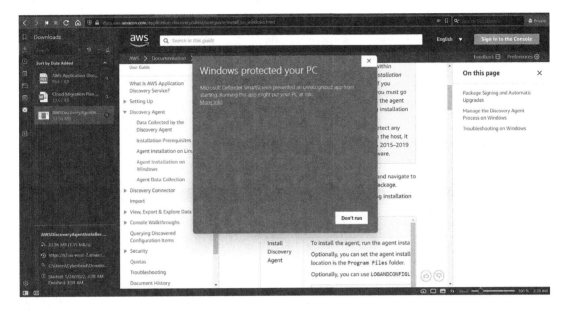

***Figure 3-17.***  *Error message pop-ups*

Most importantly is understanding the need to continue establishing permissions and creating a runbook. Figures 3-18 and 3-19 provide details of the steps taken to achieve this goal.

**Figure 3-18.** *Execution of automation document*

**Figure 3-19.** *Listed targets and parameter inputs*

Another issue you will encounter is with Amazon Athena, which may deny access to data exploration. Figure 3-20 provides an example of the dashboard.

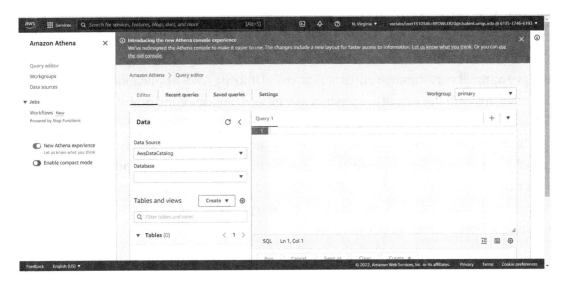

***Figure 3-20.*** *Amazon Athena data source*

Accessing this system will help you understand encryption settings and access saved queries and recent queries. Figure 3-21 provides an example of the CloudFormation of stacks created.

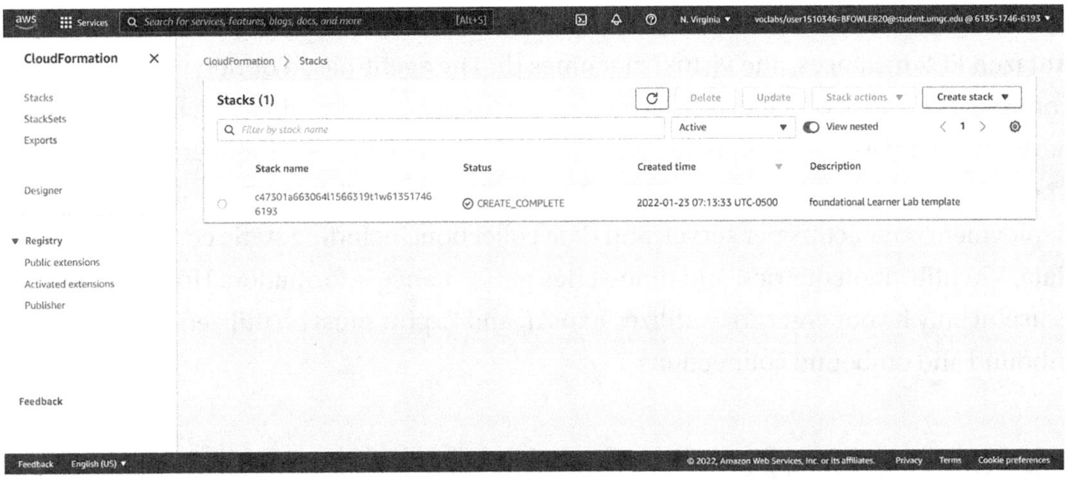

***Figure 3-21.*** *CloudFormation stack completion*

# AWS Application Discovery Service

AWS Application Discovery Service is a reliable service that enables any enterprise to achieve optimal performance and manage cost. Utilizing AWS Application Discovery Service helps with the migration process as well as decreases concerns of security risk and vulnerabilities. Most importantly, AWS Application Discovery Service offers continued support throughout the migration of the on-premises data center to the virtual environment. For example, migration for BallotOnline was exceptionally performed and met the needs of BallotOnline and their concerns. However, there is more to understanding AWS Application Discovery Service, such as understanding the agent-based option and agentless option.

## Agent-Based Option

The agent-based option is an AWS software any enterprise can install on on-premises servers and VMs targeted for discovery and migration. In fact, agents can capture system configuration, system performance, any running processes, and all details of the network connection between systems. Furthermore, agents support both Linux and Windows operating systems, which enables you to deploy them on physical on-premises servers, Amazon EC2 Instances, and virtual machines [2]. The agent-based option compiles static configuration details, including time-series system performance data and inbound and outbound network connection data, and provides data of processes that are running [3]. The agent-based option supports both VMware virtual machines and physical servers, deployment connectors per server, and data collection, including static configuration data, VM utilization metrics, and time-series performance information. However, this is useful only if your enterprise utilizes Export, and Export must be utilized for network inbound and outbound connections.

## Agentless Option

The agentless option is often performed by deploying AWS Agentless Discovery Connector, which I funneled with the BallotOnline VMware vCenter [4]. After the Discovery Connectors are effectively configured, virtual machines and hosts correlating with the vCenter can be identified. The Discovery Connector compiles static configuration data, including server hostnames, IP addresses, MAC addresses, and disk resource allocations. Furthermore, this connector compiles utilization data from each VM (virtual machine) and totals the average and peak utilizations from metrics, including Central Processing Unit data, Random Access Memory data, and disk input/output.

Although the agentless option provides support for VMWare connectors, it does not provide connectors for physical servers. Also, the agentless option does not support deployment per server, even though it offers connectors for the vCenter. Another difference from the agent-based option is the agentless option offers connectors for static configuration data and VM utilization metrics, but it does not offer time-series performance data, even with Export; nor does it offer network inbound and outbound connectors. Lastly, the agentless option does not offer connectors for running processes.

# Evaluation of Discovery Application and Infrastructure Data

AWS Application Discovery Service manages infrastructure data, including static configuration data as well as server hostnames, IP address, MAC addresses, CPU allocation, "network throughput, memory allocation, disk resource allocations, and DNS servers" [5]. In addition, CPU usage and memory are also collected. The AWS Application Discovery Agent renders clarity regarding server workloads and network relationships. This is achieved by identifying network connections shared between systems [6]. In fact, disk metrics, including read and write volume, throughput, as well as allocated/provisioned and utilized capacity, are provided [7]. However, if BallotOnline utilized either the agent-based option or the agentless option, data could only be collected through the AWS Application Discovery Agent when connected to the Internet. Moreover, it is important to understand that data can be imported from your enterprise on-premises servers and applications into AWS Migration Hub, enabling you to track the status of application migrations. This enables you to download the CSV template and upload the template using the Migration Hub import console. Keep in mind that all data collection files are formatted in CSV file format.

# Migration Recommendations

Utilizing the public cloud service requires an enterprise to align its practices and cloud policy with the recommended guidelines the US federal government established. After all, "federal laws and guidance specify requirements for protecting federal systems and data" [8]. This includes systems used or operated by a contractor or another organization on behalf of a federal agency, including cloud computing. In fact, it is essential to know that Congress enacted the Federal Information Security Management Act of 2002 (FISMA) to strengthen the security of federal information and information systems within federal agencies [9]. Thus, it is recommended private sector entities effectively develop risk-based policies and procedures that can be cost effective and reduce risk to information assets and assure focus is given to information security and information system life cycles as they work in alignment to fulfill the needs of the enterprise.

Furthermore, it was recommended that private sector entities conduct effective tests and audits to assure their usage of external cloud computing software, infrastructures, and platforms is rendering effective information security, testing of management, and operational and technology controls. Plus, it is recommended that an effective strategy is deployed to plan, implement, evaluate, and document remedial actions that can address potential deficiencies that can exist with information security policies, procedures, and practices of any enterprise [10]. Thus, the following federal policies should be evaluated prior to implementing your enterprise's cloud migration process:

- NIST SP 500-291 Cloud Computing Standards Roadmap

- NIST SP 800-144 Guidelines on Security and Privacy in Public Cloud Computing

- NIST SP 800-210 General Access Control Guidance for Cloud Systems

- NIST SP 800-146 Cloud Computing Synopsis and Recommendations

It is also recommended that your enterprise considers evaluating AWS Migration Hub. After all, AWS Migration Hub delivers acceleration programming, such as rendering consulting support, training, and service credits to lower any risk associated with migrating to the cloud, as well as helps create a stronger operational framework [11]. To help the executive members and stakeholders of your enterprise understand how AWS Migration Hub can help offset cost of migration, attending a virtual database freedom workshop offered by AWS can be helpful. These workshops are virtual sessions designed to support your enterprise in making decisions about application designs and electing the appropriate tools needed to support your enterprise as well as to attain proof of concept for all projects. In fact, AWS created a podcast (see Notes) that is also easy to download, which explains new strategies to streamline cloud migration and modernization. This podcast offers recommendations that help automate analysis for AWS application portfolios. It is also recommended to analyze any running application to assess runtime environments and process dependencies [12]. Data collected during analysis is assessed against a set of business objectives, your enterprise priorities, such as license cost reduction, speed of migration, reducing operational overhead, and modernizing infrastructure utilizing cloud-native technologies.

Lastly, you will also learn that your enterprise will need to develop clearly conveyed security policy training instruction to assure all personnel understand their role and responsibilities when operating cloud-based systems. This is invaluable and supports your enterprise efforts to develop its own cloud computing policy for in-house usage. This policy is important because it helps an enterprise establish and manage password usage, including characters allowed (upper- and lowercase, symbols, or alphanumericals). This policy also provides details about updating passwords and the requirements for password updates, including who has the authorization to change passwords and how often passwords can be changed. It is also important all Application Programming Interfaces align with the business needs and objectives of your enterprise and render quality, secure, effective services your enterprise needs. Thus, taking time to assess services relied upon from AWS is essential to assuring your enterprise attains the services it is paying for.

As you have learned, staying current with federal policies that support public cloud computing services is key to staying ahead of liabilities from external clients who may deploy civil action against your enterprise later for privacy violations. Most important is conducting audits of all virtual cloud environments, quarterly or as often as needed, to assess service needs are met and assure the system is providing the services rendered. Doing so cuts cost and keeps security breaches minimized.

# Cloud Migration Prerequisites

Because AWS is not required to migrate entities, that are not registered to obtain such supporting services, secondary indexes, sequences, default values, stored procedures, triggers, synonyms, views, and other schema objects not specifically correlating to data migration [13], prerequisites are required for an effective migration. AWS recommends gaining understanding of Amazon Relational Database Service (Amazon RDS), applicable database technologies, as well as MySQL. The first prerequisite is to create an IAM (Identity and Access Management) account, which you previously did earlier. Figure 3-22 provides an example of the IAM dashboard.

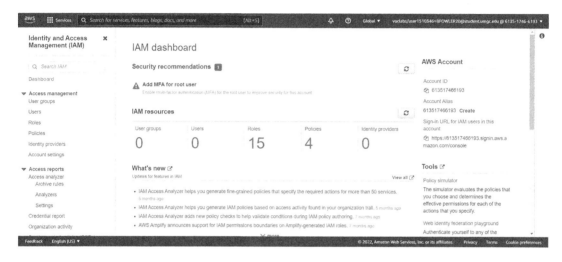

***Figure 3-22.*** *IAM dashboard*

Next, you will need to conduct research to understand the AWS virtual private cloud service and security groups as well as research about a MySQL server as a source and Amazon Aurora MySQL as a target. Learning this will enable you to understand the value of knowing the size of your enterprise target Aurora MySQL database host. Furthermore, you will need to understand the load profile of the current source SQL Server database host as well as be forced to consider CPU and memory. AWS recommends making sure enterprises have extra capacity to account for performance issues and tuning opportunities. This includes auditing, your enterprise source SQL Server database for each schema, and all additional objects encapsulated under each schema, to assess if any of the objects are no longer being utilized. You will also be required to deprecate those objects on the source SQL Server database. In fact, it is required to elect between migrating existing data only and migrating existing data and replicating ongoing changes. For BallotOnline, I elected migrating existing data and replicating ongoing changes. You may elect replicating ongoing changes, or you may need migrating existing data only. Having knowledge on what is required to manage the cloud infrastructure economically and efficiently helps enable scalability and maintain security.

# Industry-Leading Cloud Migration Approach Overview

The cloud industry migration approach recommends working with a vendor who delivers performance, security, and storage, plans for deployment, can conduct tests, and provides instructions that help an enterprise gain information on the tools and migration methods required to securely migrate on-premises to cloud. First, keep in mind that security is extremely essential because it helps deter unauthorized access to key databases and information assets your enterprise relies on. Security also reduces the impact of theft and victimization. Storage is vital to scaling up or down as needed, based on the flow of traffic volume attained any given time or day. Therefore, it is important to include these key components when planning your deployment. Having clarity on the important steps required to achieve the end goal of operating a successful migration and hosting the data securely will reduce potential security risk. Planning for deployment will enable your enterprise to acquire step-by-step knowledge of prerequisites and procedures that must be followed to achieve success during the migration, after the migration, and through the life cycle of all services rendered.

You will also need to understand the lift and shift approach to data migration and the create new approach. The lift and shift approach of migration operates best when paired with AWS Server Migration Service. Known as rehosting, this approach replicates current applications hosted in the cloud and redesigns them. This enables account holders to migrate their existing servers as well as data. The "create new" approach works with AWS Database Migration Service. The "create new" approach delivers services to design new servers in the cloud as necessary and replicates data in the cloud.

# Cloud Migration Tool Sets

Two primary cloud migration tool sets are ***AWS Database Migration Service*** and ***AWS Server Migration Service***. AWS Database Migration Service enables quick, easy, and secure migration of data sources without disruption. This service also enables all source data to continue being operational during the migration, so there is no downtime for any apps that may need to access records to operate. Additional support is rendered for homogenous migrations, as well as support for shifting data between different platforms. This is an agentless service, so there is no additional drivers or apps to install, and once migration begins, automation replicates all modifications.

AWS Server Migration Service is cost effective and helps reduce stress, but only if you are conducting a lift and shift migration. In fact, this application supported BallotOnline's retrieval of storage data from on-premises to Amazon EC2 Instances. AWS Server Migration Service also offers usage of standard IAM and provides auditing and metrics. Furthermore, AWS Server Migration Service is for lift and shift migration only. If your enterprise uses AWS EC2 Instances, this is not compatible with this service approach. Table 3-1 reports details regarding AWS Server Migration Service.

***Table 3-1.*** *Comparison of AWS Server Migration Service and AWS Database Migration Service*

| | |
|---|---|
| Console and APIs | • Standard APIs, SDKs, and CLI.<br>• Management Console operates normally. |
| Resource management | • Usage of tags or accounts<br>• Usage of EC2 launch templates<br>• Omits latency between EC2 launches of new Instance types and support of AWS MGN launch configuration |
| User management and monitoring | • Standard IAM<br>• Standard audit mechanism<br>• Standard metric mechanism<br>• Granular configurable authorization for specific APIs and AWS MGN resources |
| Control plane | • Hosted in a target region<br>• Compliant<br>• Higher availability |
| Public Internet access | • Supports a private link for replication<br>• Security benefits |
| Agentless replication | • Support provided for vCenter 6.7 and 7.0 |
| Separate accounts for staging and launching | • No |
| No rescan on reboot | • No |
| Operating system support | • Does not support Windows Server 2003 32-bit or Windows Server 2008 32-bit |
| Security | • Configured and aligned with AWS policies |
| Availability | • No dependency on other regions |

In addition, AWS Database Migration Service only supports the development of new servers in the cloud, but does not support lift and shift migration. This service delivers encryption and supports usage of Secure Sockets Layer (SSL). Most importantly, this tool provides endless backup of hardware and software as well as provides software patching and error reporting. Table 3-2 conveys the adaptability, cost, supporting services, backup support, and security of AWS Database Migration Service.

***Table 3-2.*** *Comparison of AWS Server Migration Service and AWS Database Migration Service*

| | |
|---|---|
| Adaptability | • Can scale up or down to match workload |
| Pricing | • Pay-as-you-go model<br>• Cost effective |
| Supporting services | • Endless support of migrating hardware, software, software patching, and error reporting |
| Backup support | • Endless backup support for all services and data stored |
| Security | • Encryption with AWS Key Management Service encryption<br>• SSL encryption available |

Thus, it is recommended to utilize AWS Database Migration Service because this service is easy to deploy. Utilizing this model enables increased-security policies to be implemented as well as continued accessibility of AWS Management Console. This also reduces concerns about data theft or unauthorized access to data and/or data modification. After all, because AWS Database Migration Service utilizes standard IAM, prerequisite requirements are needed to establish integration and usage of AWS OpsWorks Stacks, Chef, Automate, or Puppet Automate. In addition, AWS Database Migration Service utilizes standard audit and metric mechanisms. This is top-tier service dependency that enables access 24/7.

# AWS Database Migration Service

Your enterprise can utilize AWS Database Migration Service to migrate your on-premises databases to and from commonly utilized commercial and open source databases, including Microsoft SQL Server, Amazon Aurora, and MySQL. This service supports homogenous migration and heterogeneous migration between different platforms. However, effective migration requires prerequisites for each model of migration. AWS Database Migration Service (AWS DMS) is a web service BallotOnline utilized to migrate data from a source data store to a target data store. These two data stores are called endpoints. Once you begin establishing the migration, you will need to create an endpoint. Figure 3-23 provides an example of the dashboard for creating an endpoint service.

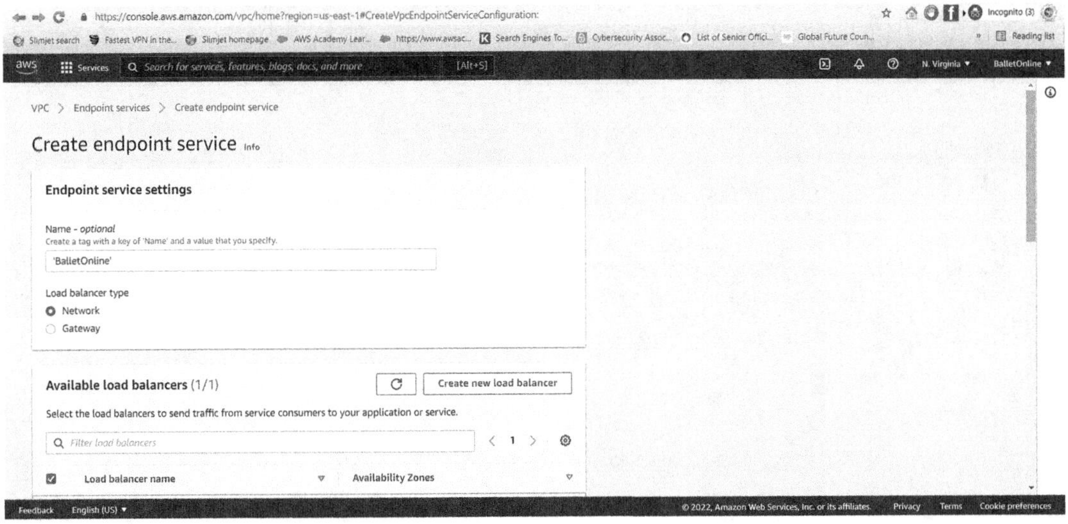

**Figure 3-23.** *Creating an endpoint service*

Next, you will need to conduct a test to assure the endpoint you created is connected to the replication Instance as required. Figures 3-24 and 3-25 provide details regarding how to classify the endpoint connection. The replication Instance name must be selected, which appears in a dropdown box. You will need to select Run test; the system will provide output, such as the endpoint identifier, replication Instance, status, and message, if any at all.

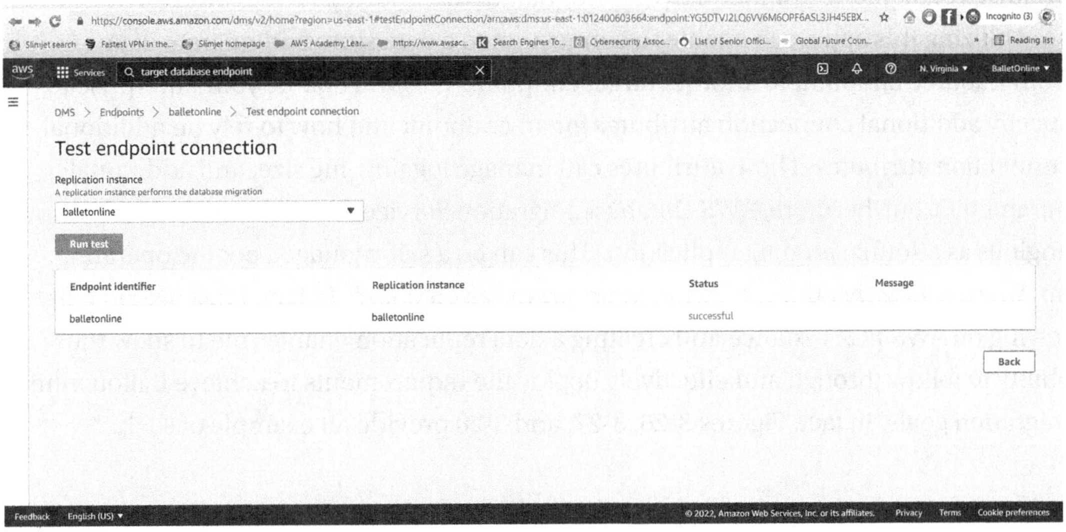

**Figure 3-24.** *Testing the endpoint connection*

***Figure 3-25.*** *Active endpoint*

Deploying this endpoint will enable you to understand how your enterprise can migrate between source and target endpoints that utilize the same database engine, such as an Oracle database to an Oracle database. You can also migrate between source and target endpoints that use different database engines, such as an Oracle database to a PostgreSQL database. The only requirement to use AWS DMS is that one of your endpoints must be on an AWS service. You can't use AWS DMS to migrate from an on-premises database to another on-premises database.

Utilizing this approach enables a connection to a data store and migrate data from a source endpoint to another target endpoint. This will enable your enterprise to specify additional connection attributes for an endpoint and how to rely on additional connection attributes. These attributes can manage logging, file size, and additional parameters. Furthermore, AWS Database Migration Service enables usage of data engines as a source for data replication. This can be a self-managed engine operating on Amazon EC2 Instance and with an on-premises database. In fact, I discovered that relying on AWS EC2 Instance and creating a data replication enables me to show the ability to follow through and effectively deploy the requirements to achieve BallotOnline migration goals. In fact, Figures 3-26, 3-27, and 3-28 provide an example of such.

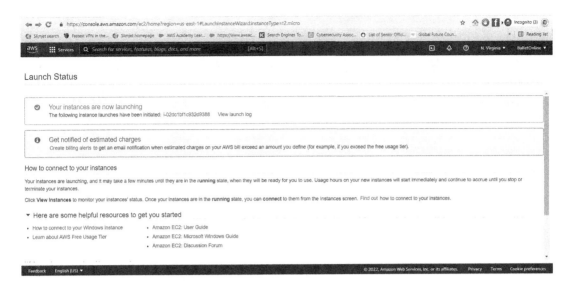

**Figure 3-26.**  *Successful Instance launch*

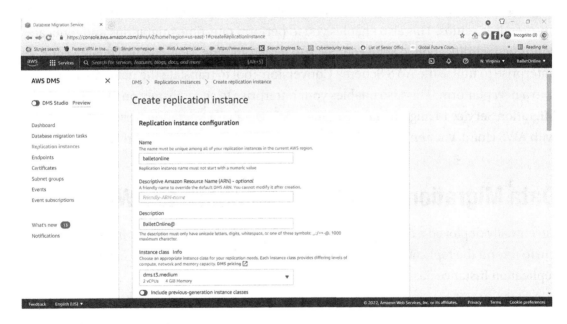

**Figure 3-27.**  *Replicated Instance*

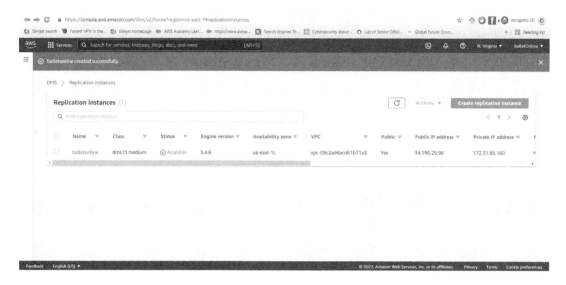

***Figure 3-28.*** *Successful running replicated Instance*

Additionally, this service helps your enterprise migrate data from the AWS cloud with on-premises setups. This also enables you to perform one-time migrations and replicate continued modification to keep sources and targets in sync. Doing so will enable your enterprise to utilize the AWS Schema Conversion Tool to translate the database schema into a new platform. This also enables your enterprise to securely rely on Database Migration Service to migrate data. Because AWS Database Migration Service is coupled with AWS cloud, your enterprise is able to attain cost efficiency and increases security.

# Data Migration of a MySQL Database to AWS

I eventually deployed a data migration of a MySQL database to AWS. Doing so enabled me to rely on the replication Instance. Figures 3-29 and 3-30 provide an example of the replication Instance dashboard.

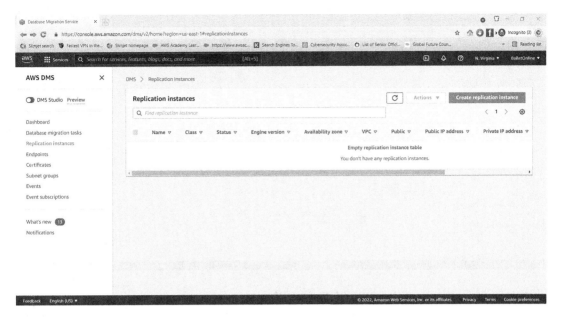

***Figure 3-29.*** *Replication Instance dashboard*

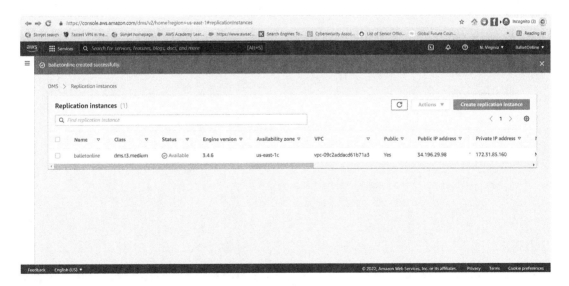

***Figure 3-30.*** *Successful replicated Instance*

Next, you will need to create an endpoint. Figure 3-31 provides an example of the dashboard.

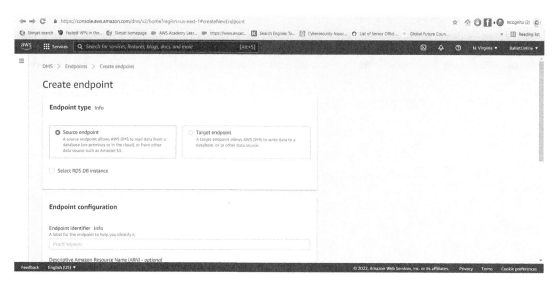

***Figure 3-31.*** *Selecting the type of endpoint*

Then, you will be required to establish database migration tasks. Figure 3-32 provides an example.

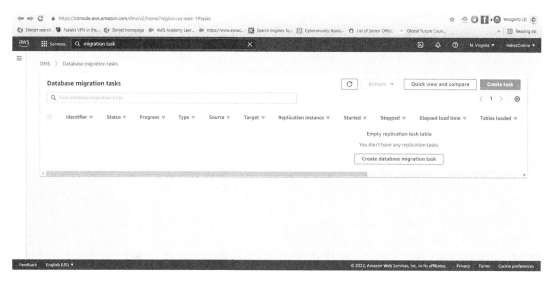

***Figure 3-32.*** *Database migration tasks*

If you are creating a new server, you will utilize the "create new" approach when utilizing AWS Database Migration Service. After all, AWS Database Migration Service is utilized to migrate data into and out of the cloud. The first reason of this limitation involves deploying development, test, or staging systems and taking "advantage of the cloud's scalability and rapid provisioning" [14]. This enables developers and testers to utilize copies of real production data as well as copy updates back to on-premises production systems.

# Cloud Migration Recommendations

A successful cloud migration requires understanding the differences in services rendered by AWS for cloud migration. Migration methodologies require a phased approach, including assessments, readiness and planning, the actual migration, and operations. Thus, it is important to understand how to effectively migrate data using migration tools and services. Taking an active responsibility to do so will enable you to understand the AWS Acceleration Migration Program, which was developed to assist organizations driven to rely on large-scale migration. In fact, AWS Managed Services enables an enterprise to migrate production workloads in a matter of days instead of months. This helps meet the needs of security and compliance requirements. However, AWS Managed Services only deploys necessary modifications as needed for private enterprise applications. In post-migration mode, AWS claims responsibility for operating the private enterprise's cloud environment. This is helpful because it supports continued migration of an enterprise's data into the cloud.

Thus, AWS Database Migration Service is easy to utilize and deploy and provides cost efficiency. Most importantly, you can reduce concern about data theft or unauthorized access to data or data modification because AWS Database Migration Service utilizes AWS IAM.

There are additional steps that must be implemented to achieve efficiency. This includes using the IAM role you previously established to enact policies and permissions. Thus, you will need to create a CloudFormation template. To do so, you will need to adhere to the AWS guide for developing a JSON template. Figures 3-33, 3-34, and 3-35 provide an example of such template development.

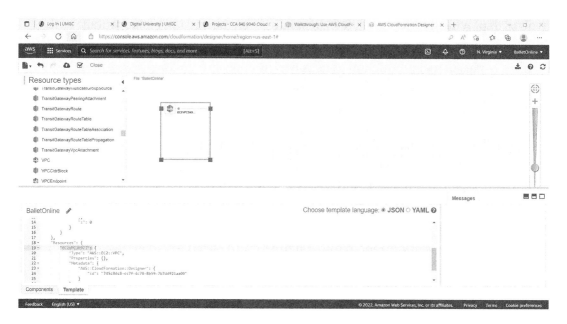

***Figure 3-33.*** *Defining the JSON template*

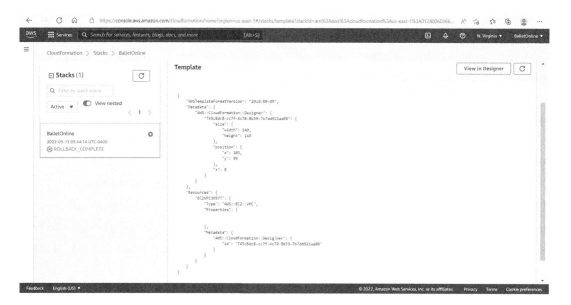

***Figure 3-34.*** *Template code*

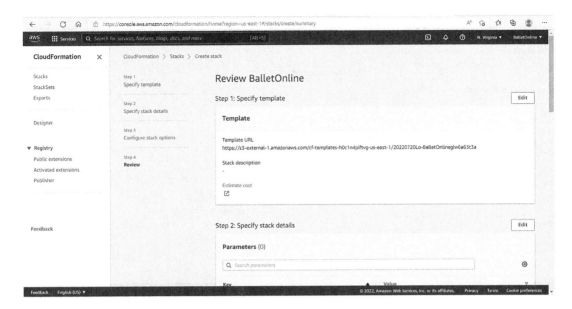

***Figure 3-35.*** *Template URL*

Next, you will create a stack and specify stack details to conduct a rollback. Figures 3-36, 3-37, and 3-38 provide an example.

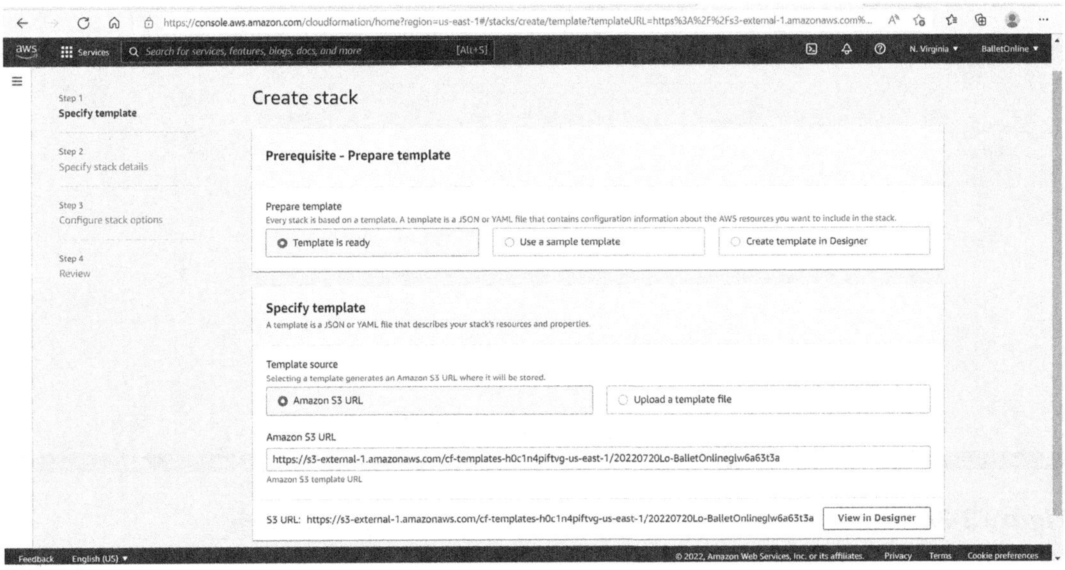

***Figure 3-36.*** *Prerequisite for a template*

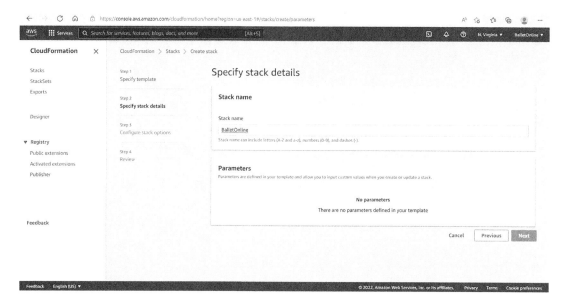

***Figure 3-37.*** *Designating the stack name*

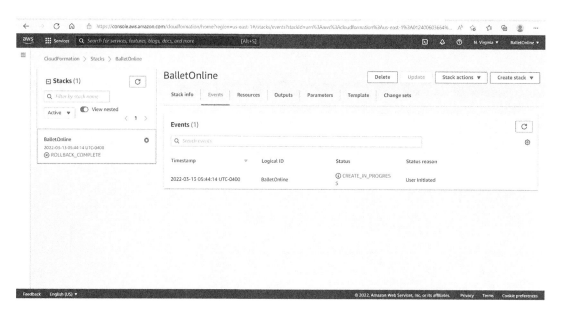

***Figure 3-38.*** *Successful creation timestamp*

# Cloud Post-migration Activities

Typical activities conducted for cloud post-migration include setting standards and controls, conducting effective monitoring and management, and focusing on performance improvement. Knowing this will help you validate and test if the data and applications migrated were successfully migrated to ensure an effective user experience is available since the move to the cloud. Doing so requires usage of CloudFormation, which enables you to validate and test if your migration was successful. Figures 3-39, 3-40, and 3-41 provide an example of the CloudFormation dashboard.

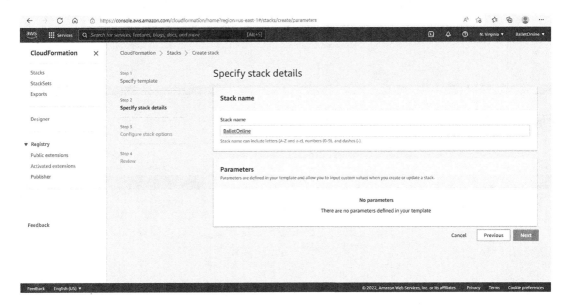

***Figure 3-39.***  *Creating the stack name*

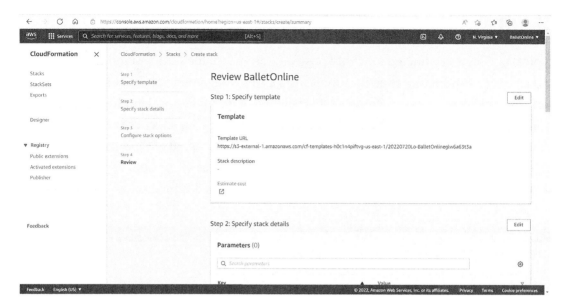

***Figure 3-40.*** *Template URL*

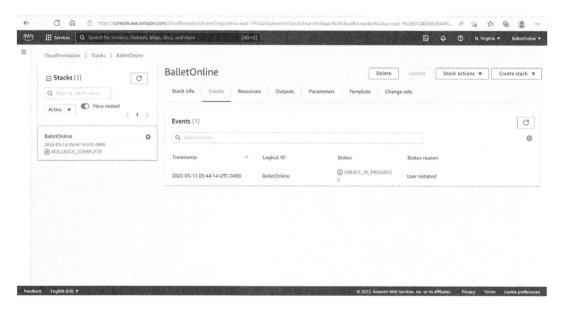

***Figure 3-41.*** *Successful progression*

You will also need to assess methods to control and optimize the infrastructure to help your enterprise manage the reduction of cost to improve security as well as increase overall performance. Relying on monitoring and management options and tools will enable you to automate IT functions required for your enterprise cloud infrastructure.

# Cloud Monitoring and Management Options

Amazon Web Services delivers two monitoring and management options, that is, AWS Trusted Advisor and AWS Systems Manager. AWS Trusted Advisor enables an enterprise to conserve budget cost and enhance security risk management that reduces cost. This automation is beneficial throughout the life cycle of your enterprise reliance of AWS EC2 Instances and VPC (virtual private cloud). This monitoring and management approach also enables your enterprise to minimize the usage of specific services that may increase usage cost. Additionally, AWS Systems Manager enables your enterprise to associate AWS resources for any purpose or activity your enterprise elects to integrate, that is, application, environment, region, project, campaign, business unit, and software life cycle. This also enables your enterprise to utilize and develop a runbook-style SSM document that helps establish the actions required to effectively perform on your enterprise's account ownership EC2 Instances.

Trusted Advisor monitors each resource with precision that cannot be compared with the eyes and hands of man. In fact, Trusted Advisor can be easily integrated to manage all enterprise services your enterprise relies on, including auto-scaling, load balancing, OpsWorks, Chef Automate, and additional services. Having this backup support reduces stress you would normally experience trying to manage services and resources your enterprise purchases from AWS, to manage and operate your enterprise's virtual private cloud infrastructure. AWS Systems Manager is also useful because it enables the deployment of policy compliance unmeasured and not provided by Trusted Advisor. Additionally, this resource oversees additional components Trusted Advisor does not. In fact, this is an additional benefit. After all, Systems Manager enables your enterprise to develop runbooks and deploy actions to safeguard the infrastructure and reduce security issues, which is a relevant concern.

Trusted Advisor will benefit your enterprise by effectively assessing the needs of all services rendered by AWS to help determine cost efficiency of services utilized. AWS Trusted Advisor deploys a scan of any AWS infrastructure your enterprise may own and compares it with AWS best practices using five categories, that is, cost optimization, performance, security, fault tolerance, and service limits. AWS Trusted Advisor makes "recommendations" on the actions your enterprise should consider deploying. Furthermore, AWS Trusted Advisor can improve the security of your AWS environment by recommending security best practices provided by security experts [15]. For example, this enables an enterprise to gain clarity regarding the identification of RDS security group access risk as well as determine if there are any exposed access keys and assess any unnecessary S3 bucket permissions. Fault tolerance also enables your enterprise to acquire information regarding improvement of services purchased, including examining auto-scaling EC2 groups, deleted health checks, and information regarding disabled availability zones and disabled RDS backups.

In addition, AWS Trusted Advisor enables your enterprise to have access to checks and guidance that provision your enterprise resources encompassing best practices to increase performance and security. Figure 3-42 provides an example of the dashboard for Trusted Advisor.

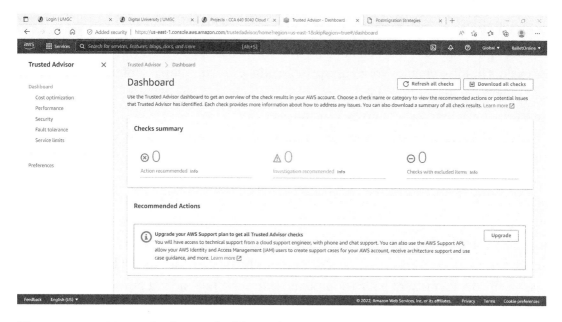

***Figure 3-42.*** *Trusted Advisor dashboard*

Utilizing this approach requires selecting an upgrade of the cost optimization to access technical support. This also requires selecting a different payment plan, instead of the Basic package previously elected. The payment plan upgrade requires a $29.00 monthly cost, which enables access to unlimited features. Figures 3-43 and 3-44 provide an example of this dashboard.

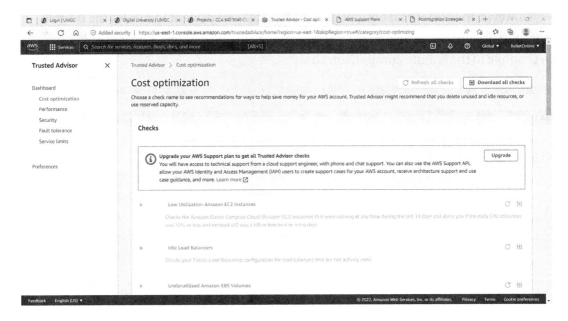

**Figure 3-43.** *Trusted Advisor cost optimization*

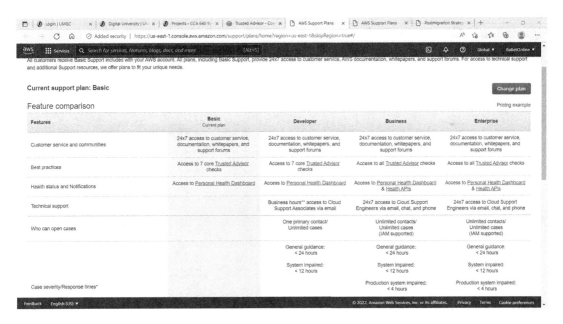

**Figure 3-44.** *Basic support plan*

However, the cost for an enterprise to utilize this component increases the overall monthly cost. So be sure to assess your enterprise's needs. Figures 3-45 and 3-46 provide an example of the feature comparison chart.

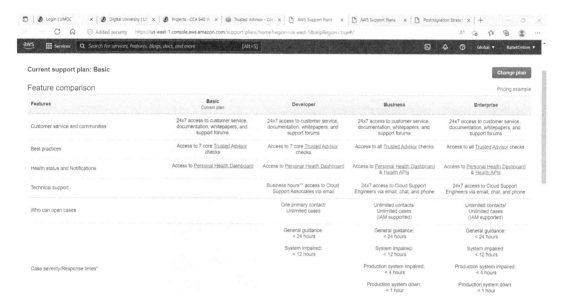

***Figure 3-45.*** *Comparison chart*

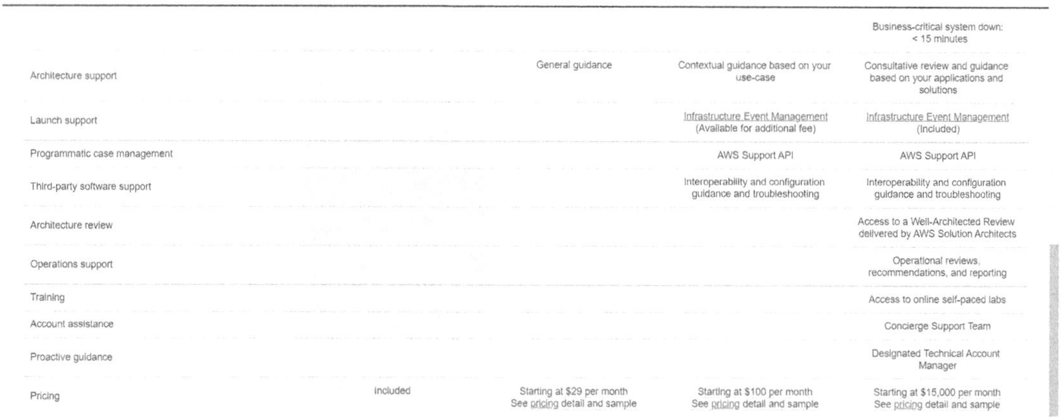

***Figure 3-46.*** *Comparison chart*

Keep in mind changing the plan from Basic to Developer will increase the cost. Figures 3-47, 3-48, and 3-49 provide an example of modifying the plan cost.

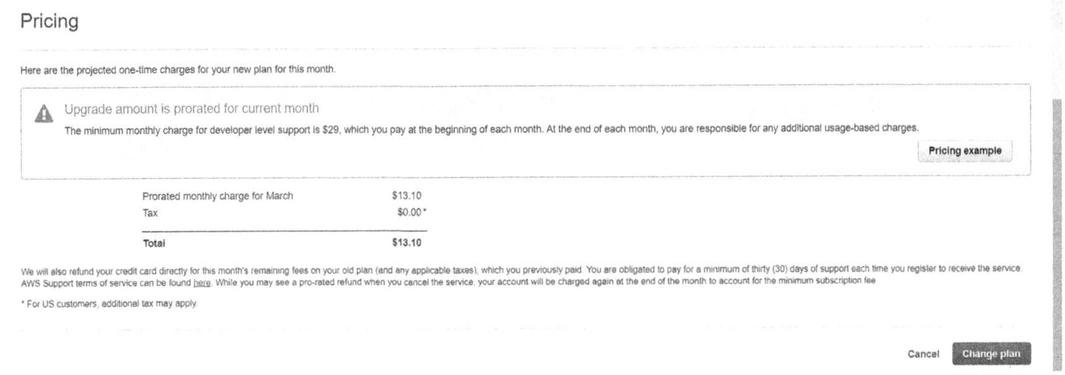

## Pricing

Here are the projected one-time charges for your new plan for this month.

> ⚠ Upgrade amount is prorated for current month
>
> The minimum monthly charge for developer level support is $29, which you pay at the beginning of each month. At the end of each month, you are responsible for any additional usage-based charges.
>
> **Pricing example**

| | |
|---|---|
| Prorated monthly charge for March | $13.10 |
| Tax | $0.00* |
| **Total** | **$13.10** |

We will also refund your credit card directly for this month's remaining fees on your old plan (and any applicable taxes), which you previously paid. You are obligated to pay for a minimum of thirty (30) days of support each time you register to receive the service. AWS Support terms of service can be found here. While you may see a pro-rated refund when you cancel the service, your account will be charged again at the end of the month to account for the minimum subscription fee

* For US customers, additional tax may apply.

Cancel    **Change plan**

***Figure 3-47.*** *Pricing for prorated cost*

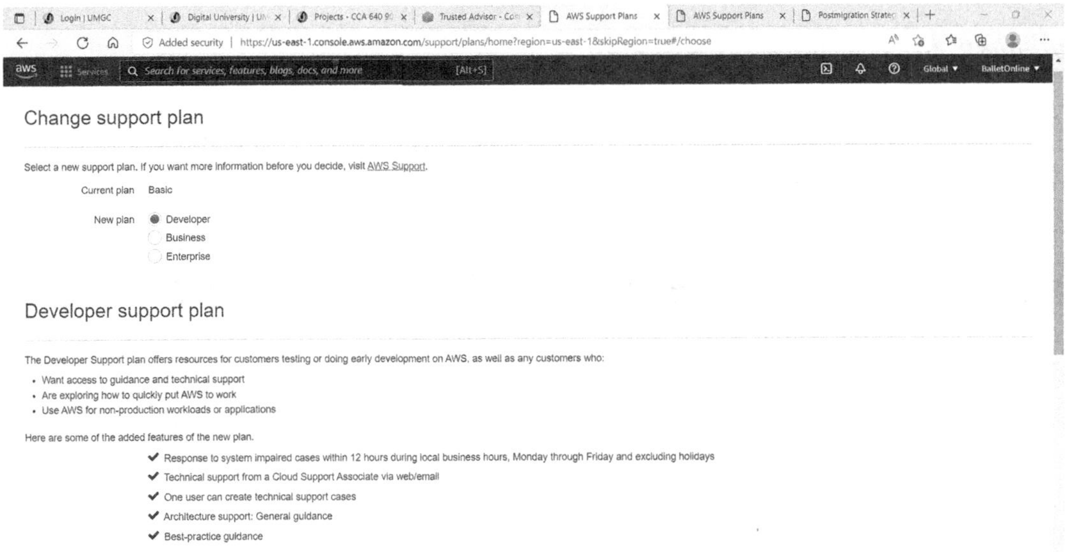

## Change support plan

Select a new support plan. If you want more information before you decide, visit AWS Support.

Current plan    Basic

New plan    ● Developer
            ○ Business
            ○ Enterprise

## Developer support plan

The Developer Support plan offers resources for customers testing or doing early development on AWS, as well as any customers who:

- Want access to guidance and technical support
- Are exploring how to quickly put AWS to work
- Use AWS for non-production workloads or applications

Here are some of the added features of the new plan.

- ✔ Response to system impaired cases within 12 hours during local business hours, Monday through Friday and excluding holidays
- ✔ Technical support from a Cloud Support Associate via web/email
- ✔ One user can create technical support cases
- ✔ Architecture support: General guidance
- ✔ Best-practice guidance

***Figure 3-48.*** *Change support plan*

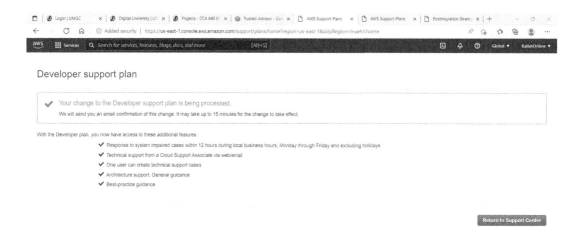

**Figure 3-49.** *Developer support plan*

Of course, you may consider utilizing fault tolerance. Figure 3-50 provides an example of the dashboard.

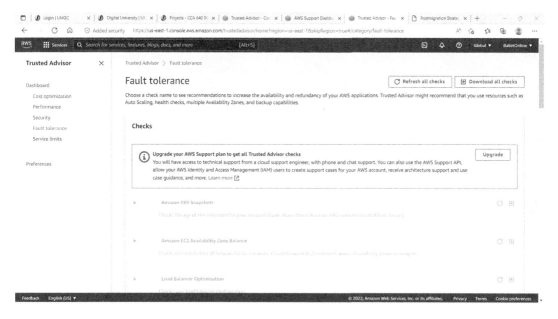

**Figure 3-50.** *Fault tolerance checks*

Next, you will need to assess the service limits, which requires selecting a check name to view recommendations for services known to utilize above 80% of a service quota. Check results utilize values based on snapshots; this enables current usage to vary. Furthermore, both quota and usage data typically take up to 24 hours to report changes [16]. Figures 3-51 through 3-62 provide examples of the service limits offered.

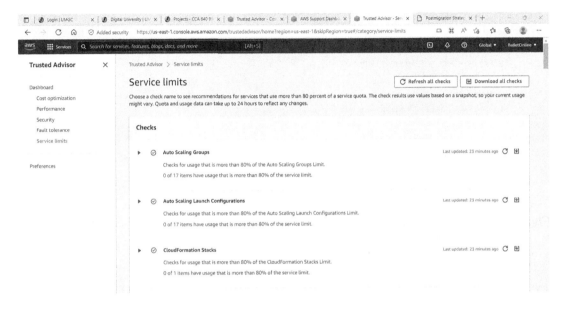

***Figure 3-51.*** *Service limits checks*

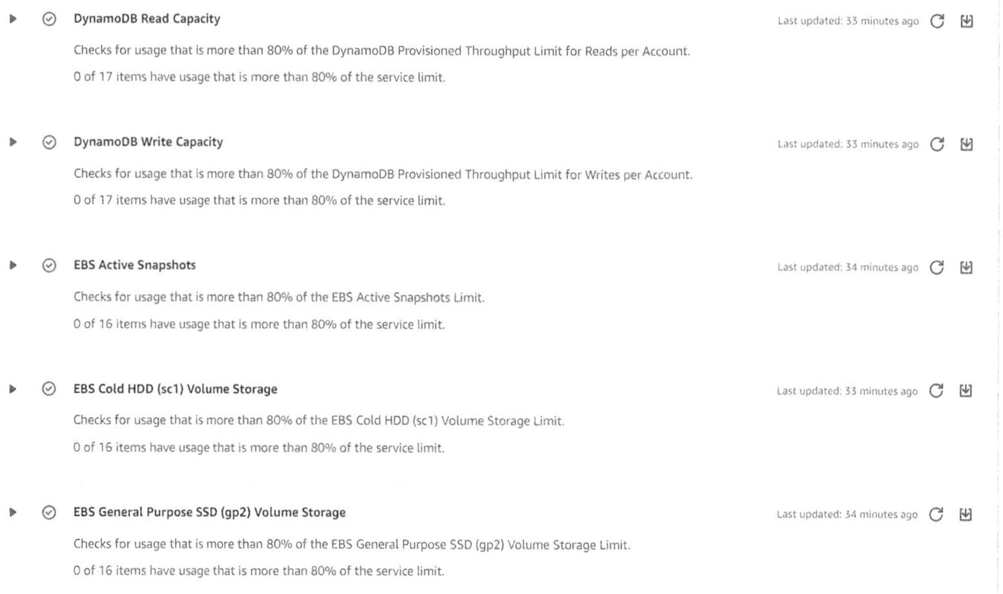

▶  ⊘  **DynamoDB Read Capacity**                                            Last updated: 33 minutes ago  ↻  ⊞

Checks for usage that is more than 80% of the DynamoDB Provisioned Throughput Limit for Reads per Account.

0 of 17 items have usage that is more than 80% of the service limit.

▶  ⊘  **DynamoDB Write Capacity**                                           Last updated: 33 minutes ago  ↻  ⊞

Checks for usage that is more than 80% of the DynamoDB Provisioned Throughput Limit for Writes per Account.

0 of 17 items have usage that is more than 80% of the service limit.

▶  ⊘  **EBS Active Snapshots**                                              Last updated: 34 minutes ago  ↻  ⊞

Checks for usage that is more than 80% of the EBS Active Snapshots Limit.

0 of 16 items have usage that is more than 80% of the service limit.

▶  ⊘  **EBS Cold HDD (sc1) Volume Storage**                                 Last updated: 33 minutes ago  ↻  ⊞

Checks for usage that is more than 80% of the EBS Cold HDD (sc1) Volume Storage Limit.

0 of 16 items have usage that is more than 80% of the service limit.

▶  ⊘  **EBS General Purpose SSD (gp2) Volume Storage**                      Last updated: 34 minutes ago  ↻  ⊞

Checks for usage that is more than 80% of the EBS General Purpose SSD (gp2) Volume Storage Limit.

0 of 16 items have usage that is more than 80% of the service limit.

***Figure 3-52.***  *Service limits checks*

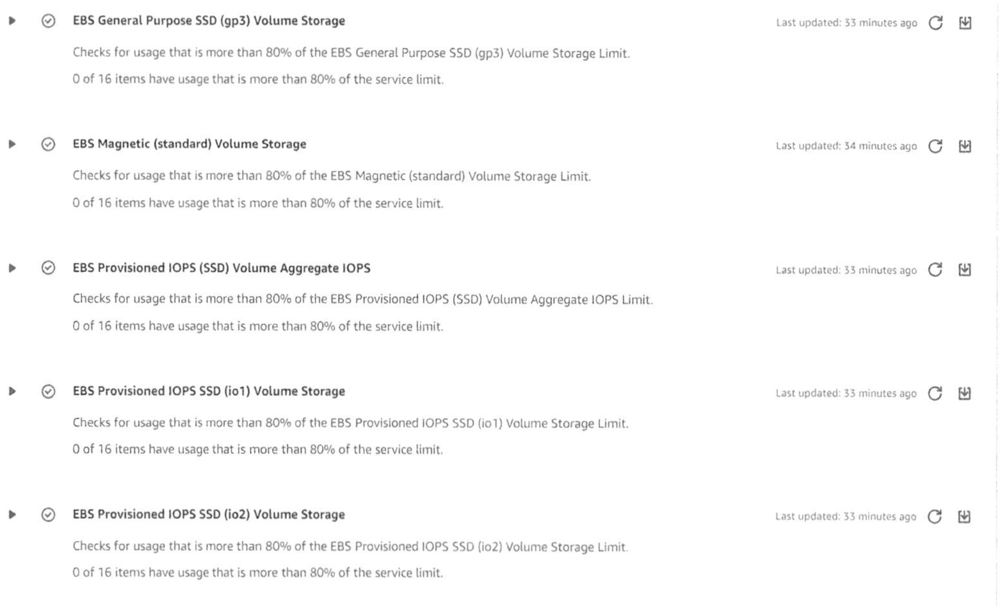

▶  ⊘  **EBS General Purpose SSD (gp3) Volume Storage**                      Last updated: 33 minutes ago  ↻  ⊞

Checks for usage that is more than 80% of the EBS General Purpose SSD (gp3) Volume Storage Limit.

0 of 16 items have usage that is more than 80% of the service limit.

▶  ⊘  **EBS Magnetic (standard) Volume Storage**                           Last updated: 34 minutes ago  ↻  ⊞

Checks for usage that is more than 80% of the EBS Magnetic (standard) Volume Storage Limit.

0 of 16 items have usage that is more than 80% of the service limit.

▶  ⊘  **EBS Provisioned IOPS (SSD) Volume Aggregate IOPS**                  Last updated: 33 minutes ago  ↻  ⊞

Checks for usage that is more than 80% of the EBS Provisioned IOPS (SSD) Volume Aggregate IOPS Limit.

0 of 16 items have usage that is more than 80% of the service limit.

▶  ⊘  **EBS Provisioned IOPS SSD (io1) Volume Storage**                     Last updated: 33 minutes ago  ↻  ⊞

Checks for usage that is more than 80% of the EBS Provisioned IOPS SSD (io1) Volume Storage Limit.

0 of 16 items have usage that is more than 80% of the service limit.

▶  ⊘  **EBS Provisioned IOPS SSD (io2) Volume Storage**                     Last updated: 33 minutes ago  ↻  ⊞

Checks for usage that is more than 80% of the EBS Provisioned IOPS SSD (io2) Volume Storage Limit.

0 of 16 items have usage that is more than 80% of the service limit.

***Figure 3-53.***  *Service limits checks*

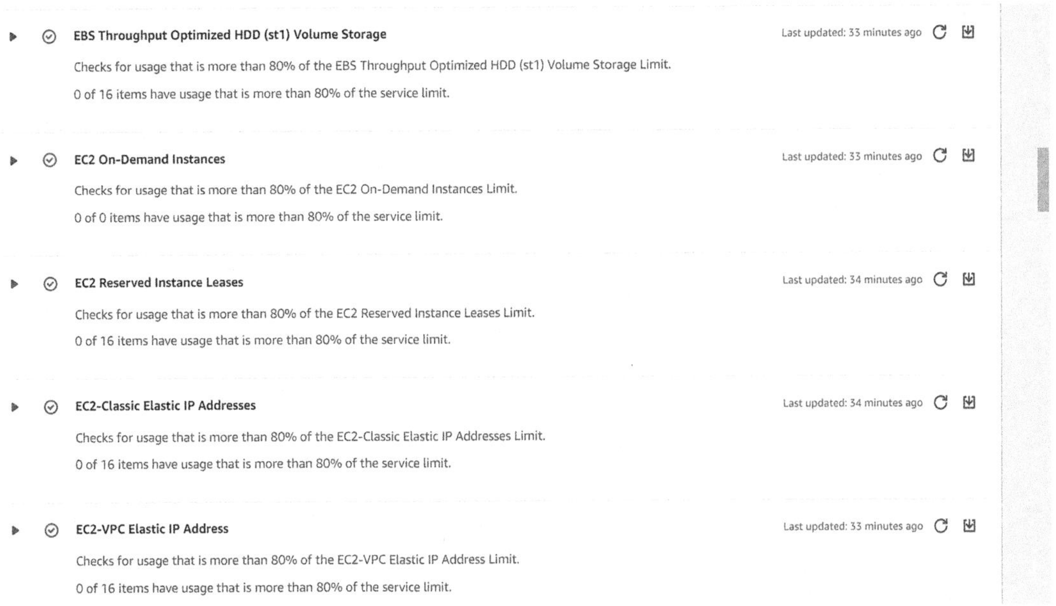

**EBS Throughput Optimized HDD (st1) Volume Storage**                Last updated: 33 minutes ago  ↻  ⊞

Checks for usage that is more than 80% of the EBS Throughput Optimized HDD (st1) Volume Storage Limit.

0 of 16 items have usage that is more than 80% of the service limit.

**EC2 On-Demand Instances**                Last updated: 33 minutes ago  ↻  ⊞

Checks for usage that is more than 80% of the EC2 On-Demand Instances Limit.

0 of 0 items have usage that is more than 80% of the service limit.

**EC2 Reserved Instance Leases**                Last updated: 34 minutes ago  ↻  ⊞

Checks for usage that is more than 80% of the EC2 Reserved Instance Leases Limit.

0 of 16 items have usage that is more than 80% of the service limit.

**EC2-Classic Elastic IP Addresses**                Last updated: 34 minutes ago  ↻  ⊞

Checks for usage that is more than 80% of the EC2-Classic Elastic IP Addresses Limit.

0 of 16 items have usage that is more than 80% of the service limit.

**EC2-VPC Elastic IP Address**                Last updated: 33 minutes ago  ↻  ⊞

Checks for usage that is more than 80% of the EC2-VPC Elastic IP Address Limit.

0 of 16 items have usage that is more than 80% of the service limit.

***Figure 3-54.*** *Service limits checks*

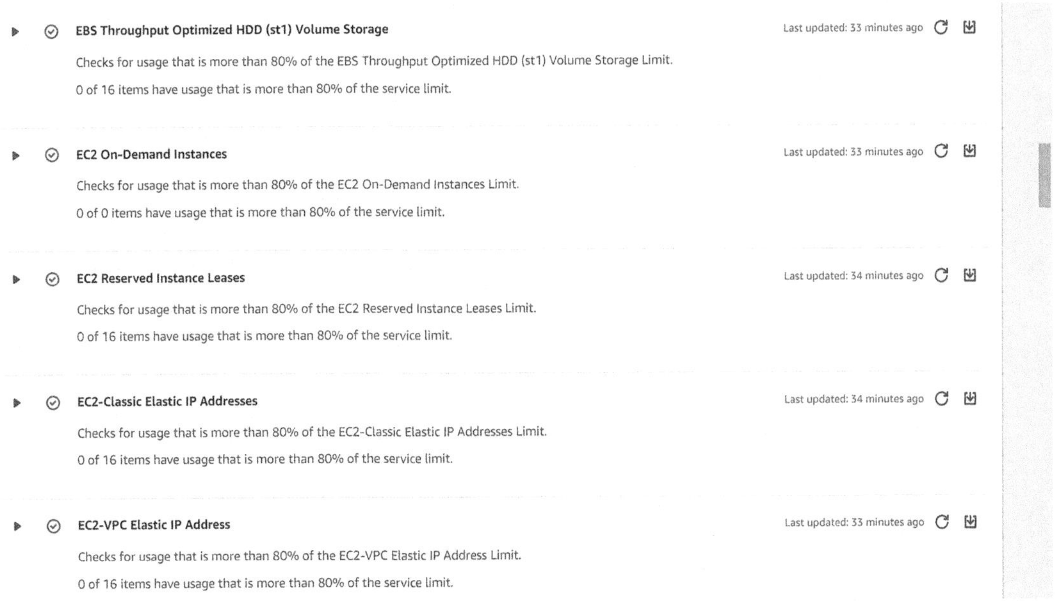

**EBS Throughput Optimized HDD (st1) Volume Storage**                Last updated: 33 minutes ago  ↻  ⊞

Checks for usage that is more than 80% of the EBS Throughput Optimized HDD (st1) Volume Storage Limit.

0 of 16 items have usage that is more than 80% of the service limit.

**EC2 On-Demand Instances**                Last updated: 33 minutes ago  ↻  ⊞

Checks for usage that is more than 80% of the EC2 On-Demand Instances Limit.

0 of 0 items have usage that is more than 80% of the service limit.

**EC2 Reserved Instance Leases**                Last updated: 34 minutes ago  ↻  ⊞

Checks for usage that is more than 80% of the EC2 Reserved Instance Leases Limit.

0 of 16 items have usage that is more than 80% of the service limit.

**EC2-Classic Elastic IP Addresses**                Last updated: 34 minutes ago  ↻  ⊞

Checks for usage that is more than 80% of the EC2-Classic Elastic IP Addresses Limit.

0 of 16 items have usage that is more than 80% of the service limit.

**EC2-VPC Elastic IP Address**                Last updated: 33 minutes ago  ↻  ⊞

Checks for usage that is more than 80% of the EC2-VPC Elastic IP Address Limit.

0 of 16 items have usage that is more than 80% of the service limit.

***Figure 3-55.*** *Service limits checks*

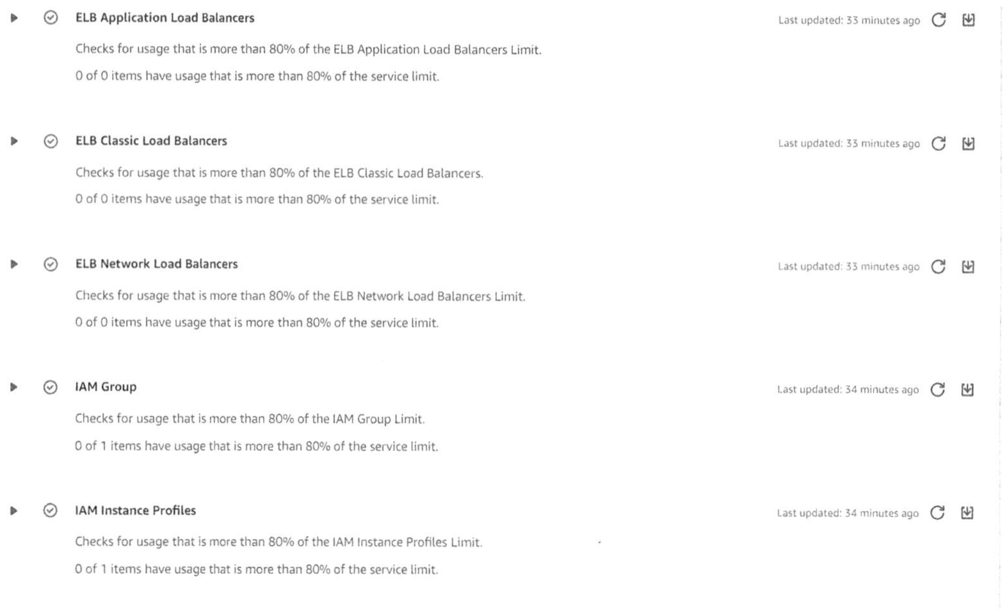

▶  ⊘  **ELB Application Load Balancers**                    Last updated: 33 minutes ago  ↻  ⤓

Checks for usage that is more than 80% of the ELB Application Load Balancers Limit.

0 of 0 items have usage that is more than 80% of the service limit.

▶  ⊘  **ELB Classic Load Balancers**                       Last updated: 33 minutes ago  ↻  ⤓

Checks for usage that is more than 80% of the ELB Classic Load Balancers.

0 of 0 items have usage that is more than 80% of the service limit.

▶  ⊘  **ELB Network Load Balancers**                       Last updated: 33 minutes ago  ↻  ⤓

Checks for usage that is more than 80% of the ELB Network Load Balancers Limit.

0 of 0 items have usage that is more than 80% of the service limit.

▶  ⊘  **IAM Group**                                        Last updated: 34 minutes ago  ↻  ⤓

Checks for usage that is more than 80% of the IAM Group Limit.

0 of 1 items have usage that is more than 80% of the service limit.

▶  ⊘  **IAM Instance Profiles**                            Last updated: 34 minutes ago  ↻  ⤓

Checks for usage that is more than 80% of the IAM Instance Profiles Limit.

0 of 1 items have usage that is more than 80% of the service limit.

***Figure 3-56.*** *Service limits checks*

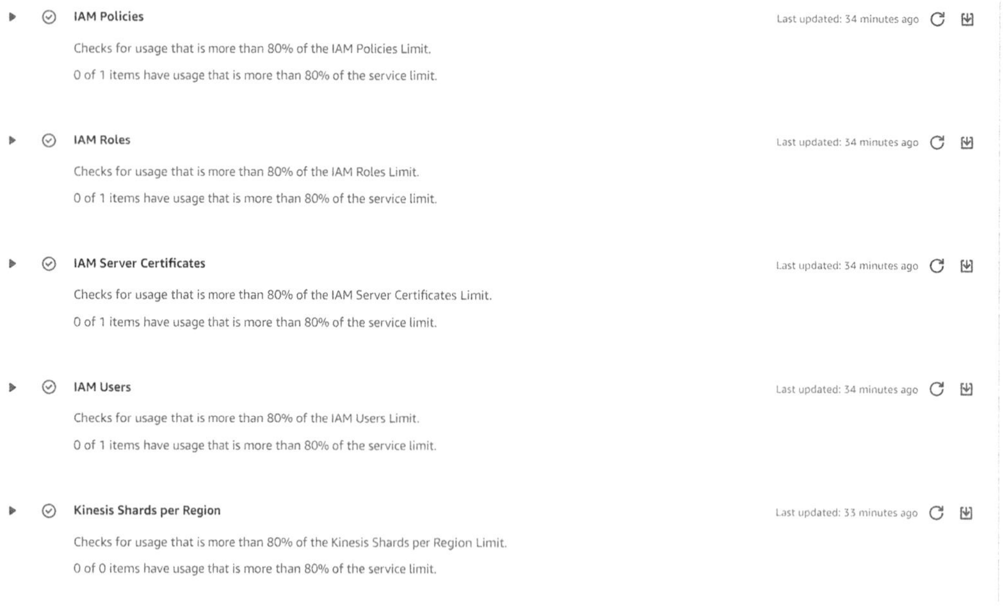

▶  ⊘  **IAM Policies**                                     Last updated: 34 minutes ago  ↻  ⤓

Checks for usage that is more than 80% of the IAM Policies Limit.

0 of 1 items have usage that is more than 80% of the service limit.

▶  ⊘  **IAM Roles**                                        Last updated: 34 minutes ago  ↻  ⤓

Checks for usage that is more than 80% of the IAM Roles Limit.

0 of 1 items have usage that is more than 80% of the service limit.

▶  ⊘  **IAM Server Certificates**                          Last updated: 34 minutes ago  ↻  ⤓

Checks for usage that is more than 80% of the IAM Server Certificates Limit.

0 of 1 items have usage that is more than 80% of the service limit.

▶  ⊘  **IAM Users**                                        Last updated: 34 minutes ago  ↻  ⤓

Checks for usage that is more than 80% of the IAM Users Limit.

0 of 1 items have usage that is more than 80% of the service limit.

▶  ⊘  **Kinesis Shards per Region**                        Last updated: 33 minutes ago  ↻  ⤓

Checks for usage that is more than 80% of the Kinesis Shards per Region Limit.

0 of 0 items have usage that is more than 80% of the service limit.

***Figure 3-57.*** *Service limits checks*

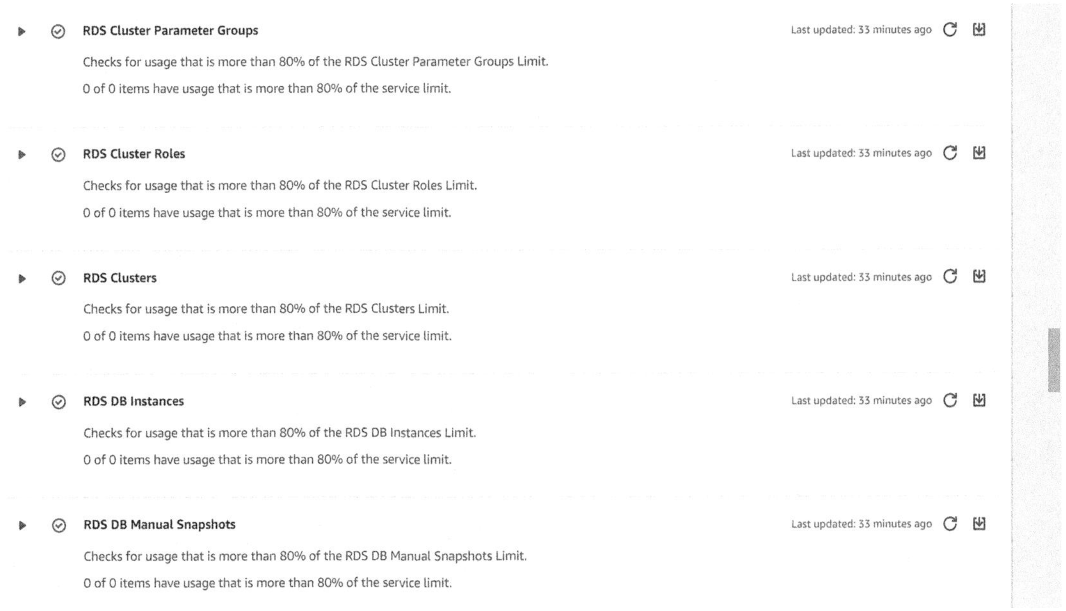

▶  ⊘  **RDS Cluster Parameter Groups**                                    Last updated: 33 minutes ago   ↻  ⊕

   Checks for usage that is more than 80% of the RDS Cluster Parameter Groups Limit.

   0 of 0 items have usage that is more than 80% of the service limit.

▶  ⊘  **RDS Cluster Roles**                                              Last updated: 33 minutes ago   ↻  ⊕

   Checks for usage that is more than 80% of the RDS Cluster Roles Limit.

   0 of 0 items have usage that is more than 80% of the service limit.

▶  ⊘  **RDS Clusters**                                                   Last updated: 33 minutes ago   ↻  ⊕

   Checks for usage that is more than 80% of the RDS Clusters Limit.

   0 of 0 items have usage that is more than 80% of the service limit.

▶  ⊘  **RDS DB Instances**                                               Last updated: 33 minutes ago   ↻  ⊕

   Checks for usage that is more than 80% of the RDS DB Instances Limit.

   0 of 0 items have usage that is more than 80% of the service limit.

▶  ⊘  **RDS DB Manual Snapshots**                                        Last updated: 33 minutes ago   ↻  ⊕

   Checks for usage that is more than 80% of the RDS DB Manual Snapshots Limit.

   0 of 0 items have usage that is more than 80% of the service limit.

***Figure 3-58.*** *Service limits checks*

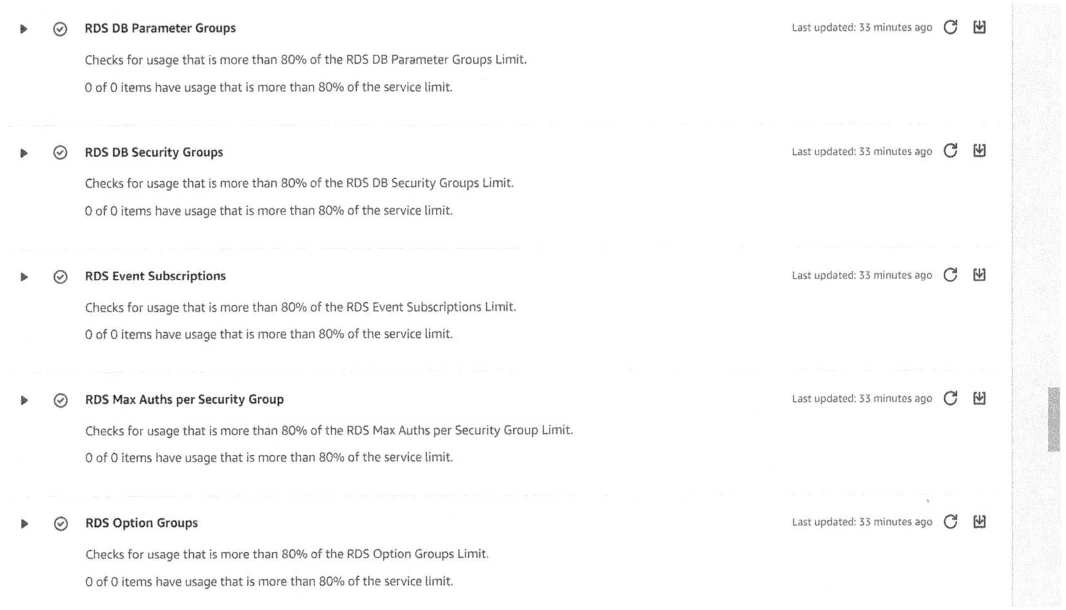

▶  ⊘  **RDS DB Parameter Groups**                                        Last updated: 33 minutes ago   ↻  ⊕

   Checks for usage that is more than 80% of the RDS DB Parameter Groups Limit.

   0 of 0 items have usage that is more than 80% of the service limit.

▶  ⊘  **RDS DB Security Groups**                                         Last updated: 33 minutes ago   ↻  ⊕

   Checks for usage that is more than 80% of the RDS DB Security Groups Limit.

   0 of 0 items have usage that is more than 80% of the service limit.

▶  ⊘  **RDS Event Subscriptions**                                        Last updated: 33 minutes ago   ↻  ⊕

   Checks for usage that is more than 80% of the RDS Event Subscriptions Limit.

   0 of 0 items have usage that is more than 80% of the service limit.

▶  ⊘  **RDS Max Auths per Security Group**                               Last updated: 33 minutes ago   ↻  ⊕

   Checks for usage that is more than 80% of the RDS Max Auths per Security Group Limit.

   0 of 0 items have usage that is more than 80% of the service limit.

▶  ⊘  **RDS Option Groups**                                              Last updated: 33 minutes ago   ↻  ⊕

   Checks for usage that is more than 80% of the RDS Option Groups Limit.

   0 of 0 items have usage that is more than 80% of the service limit.

***Figure 3-59.*** *Service limits checks*

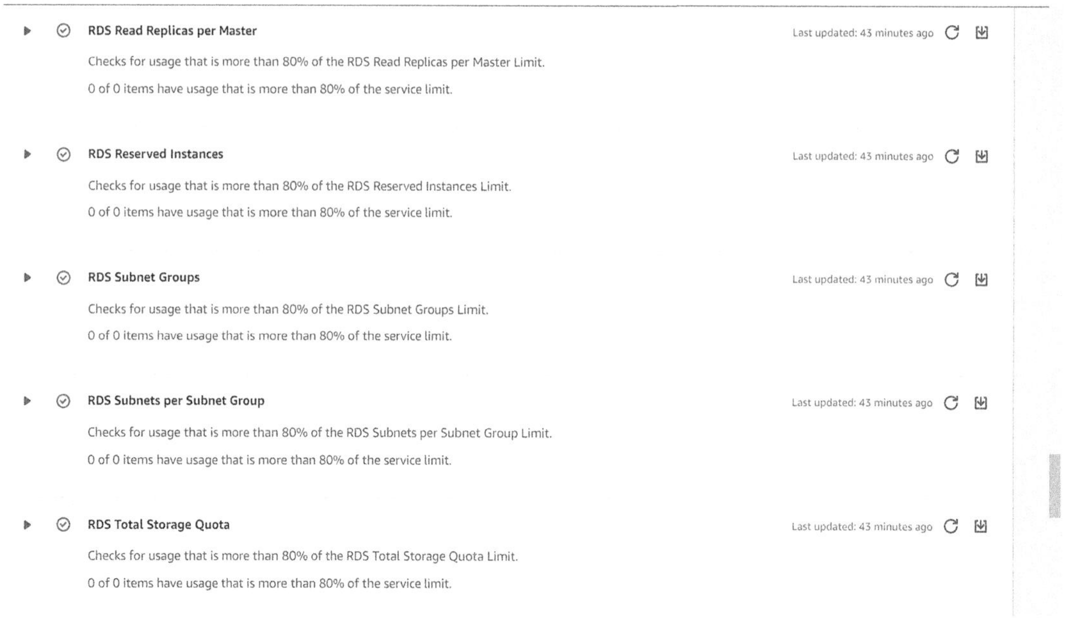

▶  ⊘  **RDS Read Replicas per Master**                                    Last updated: 43 minutes ago  ↻  ⊞

   Checks for usage that is more than 80% of the RDS Read Replicas per Master Limit.

   0 of 0 items have usage that is more than 80% of the service limit.


▶  ⊘  **RDS Reserved Instances**                                         Last updated: 43 minutes ago  ↻  ⊞

   Checks for usage that is more than 80% of the RDS Reserved Instances Limit.

   0 of 0 items have usage that is more than 80% of the service limit.


▶  ⊘  **RDS Subnet Groups**                                             Last updated: 43 minutes ago  ↻  ⊞

   Checks for usage that is more than 80% of the RDS Subnet Groups Limit.

   0 of 0 items have usage that is more than 80% of the service limit.


▶  ⊘  **RDS Subnets per Subnet Group**                                   Last updated: 43 minutes ago  ↻  ⊞

   Checks for usage that is more than 80% of the RDS Subnets per Subnet Group Limit.

   0 of 0 items have usage that is more than 80% of the service limit.


▶  ⊘  **RDS Total Storage Quota**                                        Last updated: 43 minutes ago  ↻  ⊞

   Checks for usage that is more than 80% of the RDS Total Storage Quota Limit.

   0 of 0 items have usage that is more than 80% of the service limit.

***Figure 3-60.*** *Service limits checks*

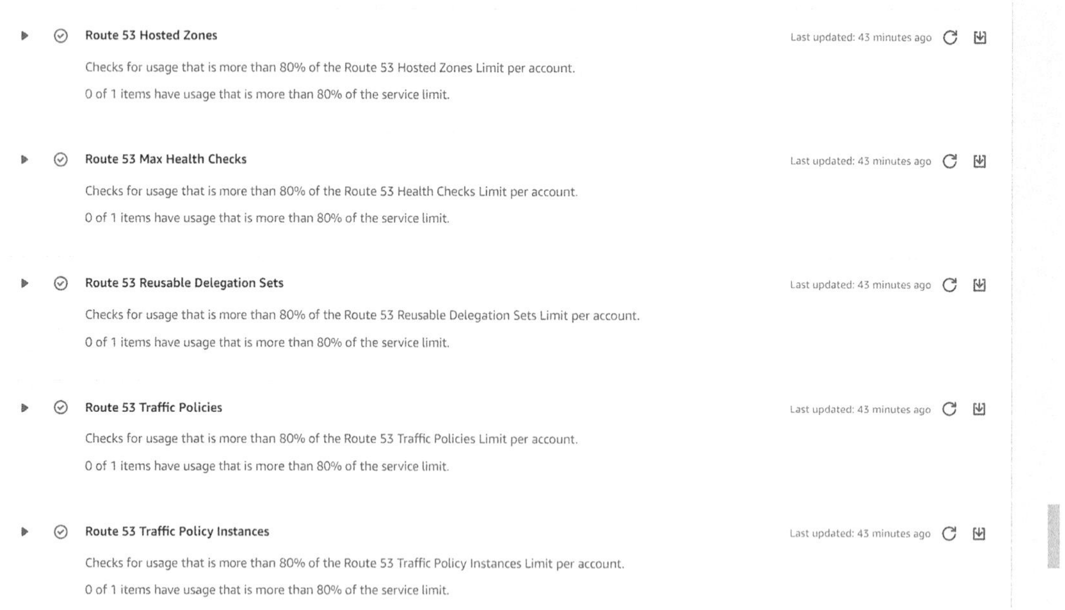

▶  ⊘  **Route 53 Hosted Zones**                                          Last updated: 43 minutes ago  ↻  ⊞

   Checks for usage that is more than 80% of the Route 53 Hosted Zones Limit per account.

   0 of 1 items have usage that is more than 80% of the service limit.


▶  ⊘  **Route 53 Max Health Checks**                                     Last updated: 43 minutes ago  ↻  ⊞

   Checks for usage that is more than 80% of the Route 53 Health Checks Limit per account.

   0 of 1 items have usage that is more than 80% of the service limit.


▶  ⊘  **Route 53 Reusable Delegation Sets**                              Last updated: 43 minutes ago  ↻  ⊞

   Checks for usage that is more than 80% of the Route 53 Reusable Delegation Sets Limit per account.

   0 of 1 items have usage that is more than 80% of the service limit.


▶  ⊘  **Route 53 Traffic Policies**                                      Last updated: 43 minutes ago  ↻  ⊞

   Checks for usage that is more than 80% of the Route 53 Traffic Policies Limit per account.

   0 of 1 items have usage that is more than 80% of the service limit.


▶  ⊘  **Route 53 Traffic Policy Instances**                              Last updated: 43 minutes ago  ↻  ⊞

   Checks for usage that is more than 80% of the Route 53 Traffic Policy Instances Limit per account.

   0 of 1 items have usage that is more than 80% of the service limit.

***Figure 3-61.*** *Service limits checks*

**SES Daily Sending Quota**                                                        Last updated: 44 minutes ago

Checks for usage that is more than 80% of the SES Daily Sending Quota Limit.

0 of 17 items have usage that is more than 80% of the service limit.

**VPC**                                                                             Last updated: 43 minutes ago

Checks for usage that is more than 80% of the VPC Limit.

0 of 16 items have usage that is more than 80% of the service limit.

**VPC Internet Gateways**                                                           Last updated: 44 minutes ago

Checks for usage that is more than 80% of the VPC Internet Gateways Limit.

0 of 16 items have usage that is more than 80% of the service limit.

> **Upgrade your AWS Support plan to get all Trusted Advisor checks**                 [ Upgrade ]
> You will have access to technical support from a cloud support engineer, with phone and chat support. You can also use the AWS Support API,
> allow your AWS Identity and Access Management (IAM) users to create support cases for your AWS account, receive architecture support and use
> case guidance, and more. Learn more

© 2022, Amazon Web Services, Inc. or its affiliates.    Privacy    Terms    Cookie preferences

***Figure 3-62.*** *Service limits checks*

You may experience Trusted Advisor Security preconfiguring four of the six components available, including Amazon EBS Public Snapshots, Amazon RDS Public Snapshots, Amazon S3 Bucket Permissions, and IAM Use. Figures 3-63 and 3-64 provide an example of such.

Trusted Advisor  >  Security

## Security                                          [ ↻ Refresh all checks ]  [ ⬇ Download all checks ]

Choose a check name to see recommendations for ways to improve the security of your AWS infrastructure. Trusted Advisor might recommend that you enable various AWS security
features, close any gaps, and examine your permissions.

> ⓘ  **Trusted Advisor checks sourced from AWS Security Hub**                                                      ✕
> You can enable Security Hub ☑ to manage and improve your security posture. You can then view your Security Hub findings as Trusted Advisor check
> recommendations below. If you're new to Security Hub or don't see recommendations sourced from Security Hub below, see the documentation ☑.

**Checks**

▶ ⊗ **MFA on Root Account**                                                          Last updated: an hour ago

Checks the root account and warns if multi-factor authentication (MFA) is not enabled.

MFA is not enabled on the root account.

▶ ⊗ **Security Groups - Specific Ports Unrestricted**                                Last updated: an hour ago

Checks security groups for rules that allow unrestricted access (0.0.0.0/0) to specific ports.

1 of 2 security group rules allow unrestricted access to a specific port.

***Figure 3-63.*** *Trusted Advisor Security checks*

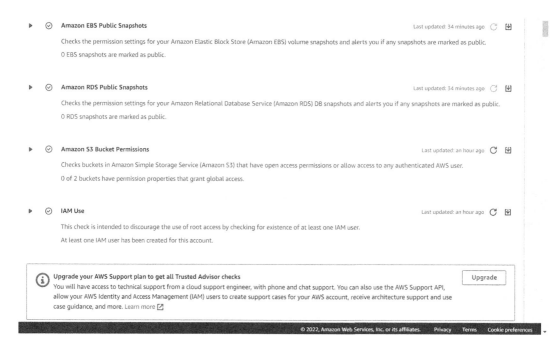

***Figure 3-64.*** *Trusted Advisor Security checks*

Lastly is Trusted Advisor Performance, which requires upgrading beyond Basic status to gain access to administrative roles. Figure 3-65 provides an example.

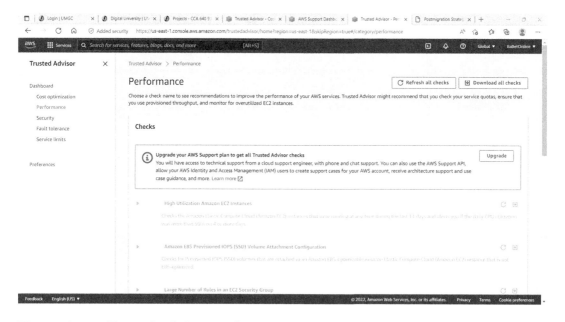

***Figure 3-65.*** *Trusted Advisor Performance*

# AWS Systems Manager Overview

Utilizing AWS Systems Manager enables your enterprise to view and manage any infrastructure being utilized. Simply utilizing the Systems Manager console enables you to view operational data from multiple AWS services and automate operational tasks between all of your enterprise AWS resources [17]. This also will enable your enterprise to effectively maintain security and compliance through scheduled scans on the nodes as well as deploy corrective steps for policy violations detected. Additionally, utilizing Systems Manager enables an enterprise to associate AWS resources by assigning resource tags. Your enterprise can assess operational data for such resources as a resource group. Relying on resource groups enables your enterprise to monitor and troubleshoot resources effectively as well as avoid potential security risks. When resources are tagged, it enables an enterprise to view any patch status on any resource posted in a Systems Manager consolidated dashboard. If problems arise from any AWS resource, you can take corrective action to correct and resolve the problem with an AWS technical support team.

Systems Manager is divided into five categories – that is, Operations Management, Application Management, Change Management, Node Management, and Shared Resources. Operations Management enables effective management of all your enterprise AWS resources. Application Management enables you to investigate and remediate issues with any AWS resource your enterprise utilizes. In fact, "Application Manager aggregates operations information from multiple AWS services and Systems Manager capabilities to a single AWS Management Console" [18]. In addition, Change Management operates as a change management framework that enables asking, approving, deploying, and reporting operational modifications to your enterprise application configuration and infrastructure [19]. Utilizing a single delegated administrator account, but only if utilizing AWS Organizations, enables an enterprise to manage changes via multiple AWS accounts across multiple regions. When utilizing a local account, your enterprise can effectively manage modifications for a single AWS account. Node Management oversees Compliance, Fleet Management, Inventory, Session Manager, Run Command, State Manager, Patch Manager, Distributor, and Hybrid Activation. However, Shared Resources depends on documentation.

# Feature Evaluation

In the AWS Systems Manager dashboard, I was able to assess how to configure Systems Manager in alignment with the needs of BallotOnline. Figure 3-66 provides is an example of the IAM dashboard I shared with you earlier.

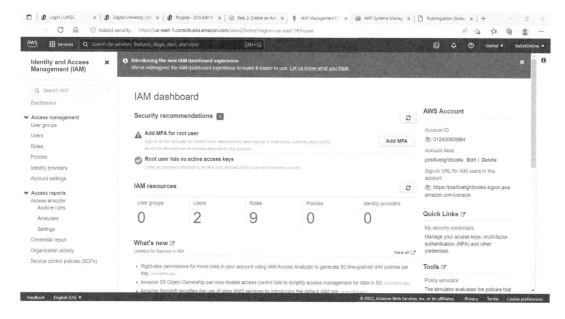

***Figure 3-66.*** *IAM dashboard*

Taking this action enabled me to add users and classify those users as Administrator, before entering a new password. Figures 3-67 through 3-70 are examples of this approach.

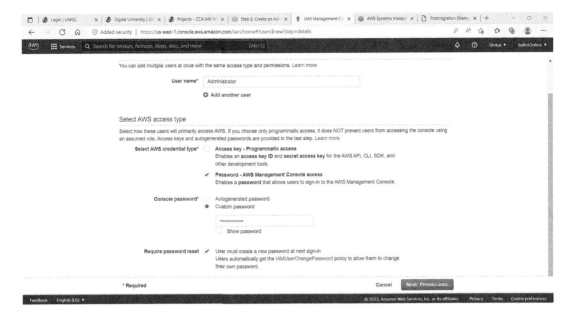

***Figure 3-67.*** *Selecting an AWS access type*

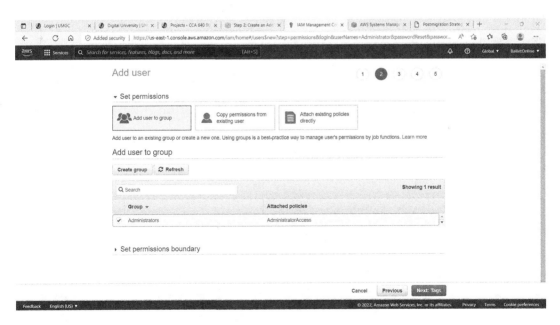

***Figure 3-68.*** *Adding users to a group*

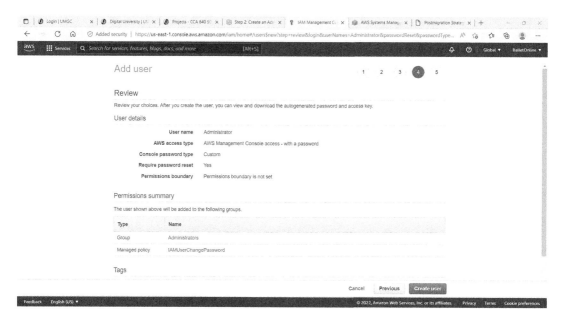

***Figure 3-69.*** *Adding user review*

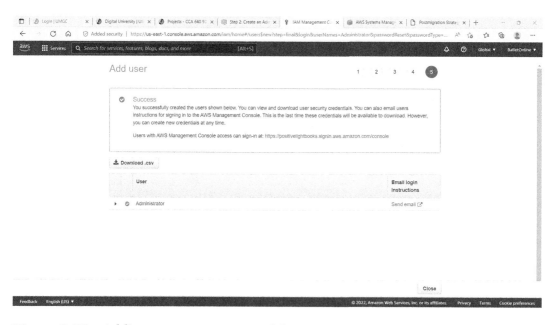

***Figure 3-70.*** *Adding user report successful*

Next, I was required to develop non-Administrator IAM users and groups for Systems Manager. Figure 3-71 provides an example of this approach.

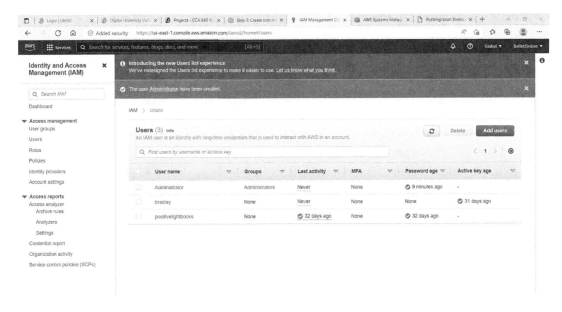

***Figure 3-71.*** *Users and groups*

Then, I was required to establish non-Admin IAM users and groups to control what resources within BallotOnline cloud infrastructure the elected non-Admin IAM users and groups can access.

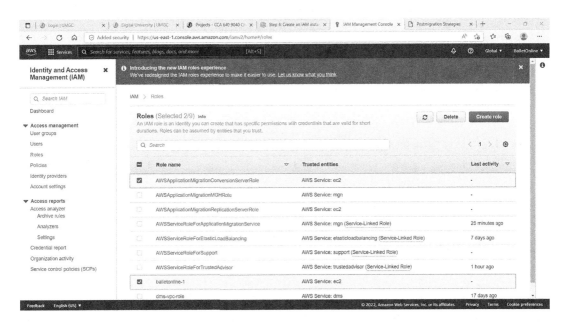

***Figure 3-72.*** *IAM roles selection*

Next, I was required to select the trusted entity, including the AWS service, EC2 Instance use case, and permissions. Figure 3-73 provides an example of these actions.

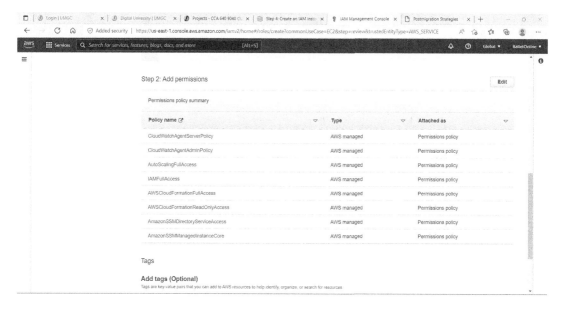

***Figure 3-73.*** *Adding permissions*

Afterward, BallotOnline roles were established. Figure 3-74 provides a proof of concept.

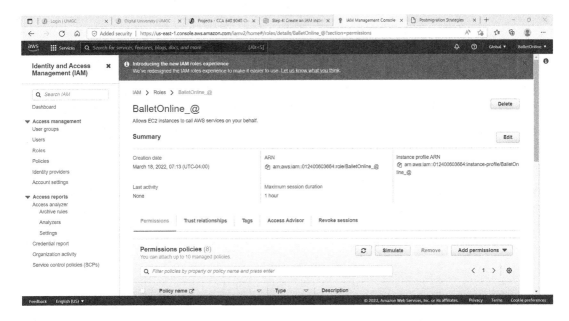

***Figure 3-74.*** *IAM for BallotOnline summary*

Additionally, I ran an Automation Workflow. Doing so enabled me to predefine automation documents and create my own, specify input parameters, select safety controls, and execute to view results. Figures 3-75 and 3-76 provide examples of the proof of concept deployed.

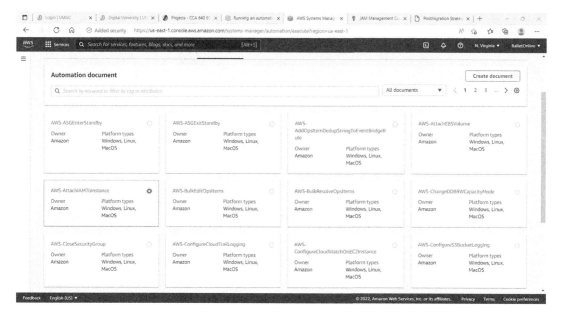

***Figure 3-75.*** *Automation document selection*

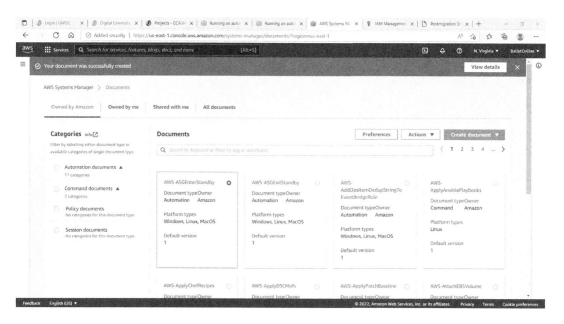

***Figure 3-76.*** *Document selection*

Then, I deployed the Automation Workflow using an IAM Service Role. Figure 3-77 provides proof of concept.

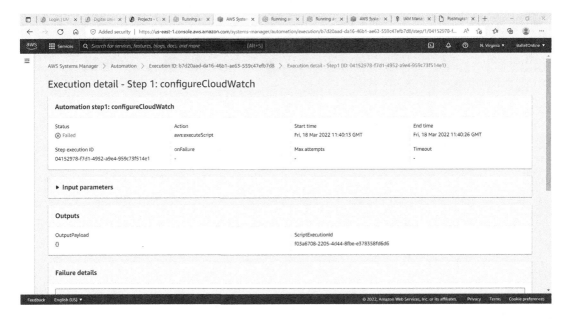

***Figure 3-77.*** *Execution detail for step 1*

However, a failure notification surfaced. Thus, I had to configure automatic updating of the SSM Agent and establish the association within Node Management to predefine SSM documents or create my own. This helped me connect BallotOnline Instances with any SSM document deployed as well as specify scheduling for a desired state and create the option to output data to Amazon S3. Figures 3-78 through 3-80 provide proofs of concept. Keep in mind your enterprise development approach will mirror many of these methods. Having this visual helps guide you through these procedures.

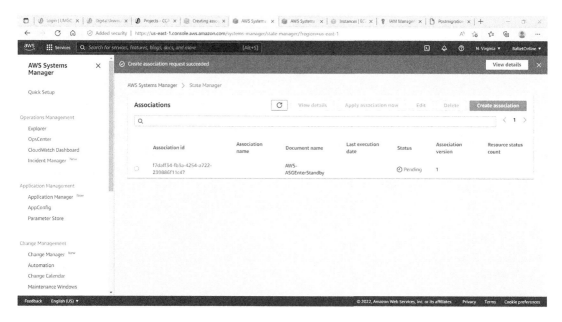

***Figure 3-78.*** *Association creation validated*

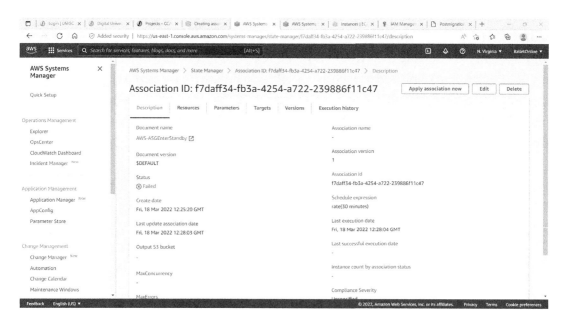

***Figure 3-79.*** *Association ID provided*

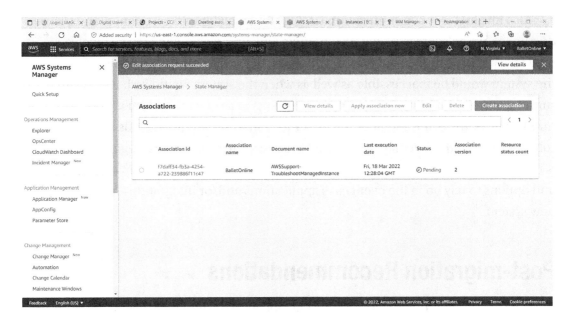

*Figure 3-80.* *Association request validated*

# Cut-Out/Rollback Options

My cut-out/rollback for BallotOnline included scheduling dates of actions to migrate and have the system up and running effectively. Thus, I designated checkpoints and discovered how to determine when a rollback might be necessary. Keep in mind that a cut-out plan should include a checklist of essential tools needed once data is transferred. This checklist includes assessing a stop on all data entering and departing from the legacy on-premises system. As the primary administrator, you are required to inform personnel to stay out of the system while the cutover is being conducted. There are also preliminary activities required to share vital details with stakeholders and educate them on every upgrade deployed to make sure everyone has knowledge of what is happening and what is being done to enable an ease of transition from the old system to the new. This includes preparing a list of tasks to be done during the transfer of data and strategies that encompass potential timelines for IT personnel teams to be aware of during the transition period. It is important to conduct tests throughout the life cycle, so timelines should be scheduled to help with effective management of the premigration and post-migration.

Also invaluable is communication strategy for email templates, memos, and secure document files to share with key stakeholders and employees who may be involved with the system. This plan enables stakeholders and end users to understand when the system would be inaccessible as well as when the system would be back up and running live. This requires integrating checkpoints to assure the system is effectively monitoring both during and after the migration. Sharing essential details about any rollback procedures that may be required to restore the system to its original parameters is important to control compliance. This includes organizational backup strategies and options to rely on in the event case applications and/or integrations fail within the new system.

# Post-migration Recommendations

Pre- and post-migration procedures must be documented and provided to the appropriate stakeholders who are instrumental in assessing improvements that may be overlooked after the migration has occurred. Keeping a written log of all activities and making sure to screen capture each phase of the development and throughout the life cycle of the project is beneficial. Doing so helps decrease human error. It is also important to back up the system once it is up and operating. This requires conducting security testing daily and maintaining written reports. Effective communication and data collection reporting helps the post-migration be a success.

# Summary

Usage of AWS Trusted Advisor and AWS Systems Manager enables an enterprise to achieve short- and long-term goals by reducing potential threats that impede operating a secure cloud infrastructure. Aligning cloud policy with the recommendations and guidelines offered by the National Institute of Standards of Technology is another important method of adding additional layers of security to your enterprise cloud infrastructure. Furthermore, having a premigration and post-migration plan is essential to being prepared to make modifications as needed, during and after the migration. However, you must also understand the value of diligently conducting system backup and archiving as well maintaining work logs with dates and timelines. These are just a few methods to remember. After all, operating a cloud infrastructure requires having knowledge of data backups and archiving to cloud using cloud sync services and AWS CloudWatch monitoring. You also need to understand AWS Service Catalog and cloud operation end users' guides and cloud operation administrative guides. In fact, Chapter 4 will provide details regarding these subjects.

# Discussion Questions

1. What type of service does BallotOnline utilize for cloud?

2. What component helps you predetermine the estimated cost of monthly usage fees?

3. What are two recommended migration tools?

4. What does a JSON file describe?

5. What five resources are associated with the IAM dashboard?

6. How many automation execution commands can you select from?

7. What is AWS Application Discovery Service?

8. What does the agent-based option support?

9. What can Discovery Connectors identify?

10. What does the AWS Discovery Agent render?

11. What does NIST SP 500-291 represent?

12. What does NIST SP 800-144 represent?

13. What are the two cloud migration tool sets?

14. What are the two load balancer types when creating endpoint services?

15. What are the nine categories for replication Instances?

16. What does deploying a data migration of MySQL database to AWS enable?

17. What are the two endpoint types?

18. Why was the AWS Migration Acceleration Program developed?

19. What are steps 1, 2, and 3 of CloudFormation?

20. How many monitoring and management options does AWS offer?

21. How can Trusted Advisor benefit your enterprise?

22. What does AWS credential type enable?

23. What two IAM roles are highlighted and selected?

24. What is the AWS Systems Manager Associations Document name?

# CHAPTER 4

# Computing Development and Management

**Learning Objectives**

Understand how to assess cloud adoption policy to align with existing enterprise policy.

Define a Growth Projection Analysis.

Understand Service Level Agreements for cloud services acquired.

Understand cloud vendor governance strategies.

With the integration of cloud infrastructure as the new information system for BallotOnline, there was a need to increase development and implementation of updated cloud policy that aligned with the existing enterprise information security policy. No longer does the existing information security policy provide instructions to deter and thwart unauthorized access to the enterprise cloud virtual private infrastructure. To be effective, the updated information security policy must provide federal-grade compliance regulations regarding usage, multi-factor authentication, and security. Therefore, it is important for you to gain clarity on how to update the current policy and define a policy that will prevent the enterprise from liability cost. Operating offices in various geographical locations require trust and assurance in both management and personnel, overseeing enterprise technology tools hosting encrypted data sources. Thus, policy must be developed to include all branches of information technology, information systems, and cloud virtual private infrastructure to govern those responsible for developing, implementing, and managing the enterprise's information assets. In this chapter, you will acquire knowledge regarding the policy scope and how this needs to align with existing IT policies within your enterprise. Furthermore, you will review the business and technical impact analysis I conducted on behalf of BallotOnline to help you develop your own business and technical impact analysis and learn how to develop

107

© Bradley Fowler 2023
B. Fowler, *AWS for Public and Private Sectors*, https://doi.org/10.1007/978-1-4842-9048-4_4

an exit strategy from an on-premises system to a virtual private cloud. Next, you will learn how to evaluate a cloud service for email and email in the cloud, evaluate cloud service offering for software development and design for Software Development Kits in the cloud, and evaluate cloud services for backups and archiving and architecture design for backups and archiving in the cloud. Additionally, you will acquire knowledge about cloud monitoring solutions for backup and archiving and gain knowledge regarding the AWS virtual private cloud, virtual private network, and AWS S3 bucket. As an added bonus to this chapter, you will gain knowledge regarding cloud synchronization services and data backup and archiving to cloud, using a cloud sync service and AWS Service Catalog. AWS Service Catalog includes details about cloud operations end user guide, cloud operations administration guide, configuration and deployment of AWS Service Catalog, as well as the limitations.

# The Policy Scope

BallotOnline's current IT policy encompassed details regarding current technology tools and systems relied on daily to enable the enterprise to deploy business operations with little impact and concern of security risk or reputation damage. However, since the legacy system was outdated, this placed the enterprise at risk of being incapable of competing with competitors and acquiring the leverage needed to excel and increase stakeholders' investments while increasing consumer trust in the quality of services they sought from BallotOnline. In fact, BallotOnline's legacy system currently included computers, hardware, software applications, and telecommunications, which was instrumental in managing services delivered through BallotOnline enterprise's operations. Thus, integrationg cloud services for BallotOnline, required IT policy to be modified to include details about the proposed virtual private cloud environment as well as explain how to decrease unauthorized threats to daily engagement of business operations that typically aid in creating vulnerabilities known to impact a legacy system, that is, human error, Distributed Denial of Service Attacks, cyber-attacks, malware, and ransomware attacks. Therefore, modifications for your enterprise information security policy should include cloud-ready applications for email, software development, backup, and archiving. Furthermore, all IT and cloud policies should align with the recommendations and guidelines established by the National Institute of Standards and Technology, regarding security methods for information technology, information systems, cloud systems, email, software, backup, and archiving.

# Aligning Cloud Usage with Existing IT Policies

An enterprise cloud usage and security policy must include multi-factor authentication and access authorization. Attention should focus on including the development of the virtual private cloud, such as planning, development, deployment, and management. Implementing a hierarchy governance enables an enterprise to delegate management to oversee cloud usage and security with AWS, with little downtime and risk associated with unauthorized access to essential components within the selected cloud environment, that is, Instances, ports, and keypairs. Therefore, your enterprise information security compliance policy needs to align with the National Institute of Standards and Technology SP 800-53 recommendations for Security and Privacy Controls for Federal Information Systems and Organizations. Doing so enables the enterprise to rest assured such recommendations will increase security and decrease stress of noncompliance. Defining an internal security policy that regulates the security of all technology tool assets should conform to the standards set by the industry.

In fact, it is invaluable to update the existing IT policy for email. Doing so will help align the IT and cloud policy with NIST SP 800-45, which covers Guidelines on Electronic Mail Security, as well as SP 800-177 for Trustworthy Email and SP 800-144 for Guidelines on Security and Privacy in Public Cloud Computing. Cloud usage and security policy modification alignments need to also include details about usage and management of intrusion detection and prevention software applications. These tools are instrumental in helping decrease unauthorized access to vulnerable systems hosting sensitive information assets.

Another policy modification should include software development. Your enterprise can align with recommendations and guidelines of NIST SP 800-160 Systems Security Engineering and NIST SP 800-218 Secure Software Development Framework. Doing so will enable the enterprise to maintain information on current trends in detecting and preventing software development vulnerabilities and security issues. Additional modification should include requirements for backup and archiving. Enterprise cloud usage and security policy should also align with the recommendations in NIST SP-800-171A Assessing Security Requirements for Controlled Unclassified Information for backup compliance and archiving.

Furthermore, it is important to evaluate IT policy relating to recovery time objectives, which focuses on a scale of the amount of time required to recover an application once a disaster strikes. Thus, it is imperative to factor in determining a data backup plan. As a result, it was recommended BallotOnline consider relying on multiple cloud environments that could support a system backup in the event there was a system disaster or utility interference that created a power outage. As a result, recovery point objectives should be assessed to acquire clarity on the amount of acceptable data loss if an outage or if a disaster event occurs. There should also be consideration of cost for change because this enables your enterprise to assess the economic impact that may occur when the infrastructure components or IT operations are modified from business as usual. In fact, it's invaluable to always consider the cost of change when deploying a total cost of ownership of any new product or service.

# Growth Projection Analysis

Defining a Growth Projection Analysis requires forecasting the future needs of the enterprise. Each enterprise GPA will align with the unique needs, including the number of users and servers needed to conduct business, both in a physical work environment and virtual, as well as knowing the estimated number of network switches required and the number of terabytes for data storage. Thus, the proposed Growth Projection Analysis provided in Table 4-1 delivers details regarding 2018/2019 and 2020/2021, which shows an increase by 10% for users and servers. The network switches were calculated using a TCP Throughput Calculator, and the data storage amount was added based on previous usage. You should allow room for error in calculations when defining your enterprise

Growth Projection Analysis.

# Historical Infrastructure Growth Trends at BallotOnline

***Table 4-1.*** *A list of infrastructure elements*

| Infrastructure Elements | 2012/2013 | 2013/2014 | 2014/2015 | 2015/2016 | 2016/2017 | 2018/2019 | 2020/2021 |
|---|---|---|---|---|---|---|---|
| Users | 150,000 | 250,000 | 650,000 | 750,000 | 1,500,000 | 1,650,000 | 1,815,000 |
| Servers (standalone physical and virtual) | 75 | 150 | 400 | 550 | 1,100 | 1,210 | 1,331 |
| Network switches | 4 | 8 | 15 | 18 | 30 | 34 | 38 |
| Data storage | 200 TB | 400 TB | 850 TB | 1 PB | 2.5 PB | 4 PB | 4.5 PB |

Managing the Growth Projection Analysis for your enterprise effectively helps control budget spending.

# Service Level Agreements in the Cloud

Working in partnership with cloud service providers includes comprehending the Service Level Agreements that entangle enterprises in litigation that is costly and prevents customers from unleashing themselves from the contracts they sign with service providers because customers neglect to thoroughly review the content conveyed in the SLA. Luckily, AWS provides access to the SLA to help you gain understanding of the key elements within the SLA. In fact, you can gain direct access to this website at the following link: www.aws.amazon.com/ec2/sla/historical/.

Thus, key services and Application Programming Interfaces your enterprise should gain knowledge about when partnering with AWS cloud environment services include Amazon Elastic Compute Cloud (Amazon EC2). Amazon guarantees quality products and services monthly at least 99.99% in each use case within the billing cycle. If the services rendered do not meet your enterprise expectations, the enterprise will receive a Service Credit as detailed in the SLA. Furthermore, the SLA covers protection on all "regions," including Instances relied on that may not be operating as expected across all regions. For example, if Region 1 Instances are operating as expected, but Region 3 Instances are down for a period, the SLA guarantees compensation for that downtime. The SLA also explains how credits are rendered for charge backs when Instances are not operating effectively. The SLA outlines detailed steps your enterprise needs to take to acquire these credit payments. Details also convey actions that must be taken immediately when downtime is discovered. However, Amazon will not cover downtime of Instances due to Internet outages incurred by end users. To avoid this issue, your enterprise is required to maintain efficient Internet services that guarantee little downtime and/or service interruption. Furthermore, the SLA is a policy including details regarding AWS EC2 and each individual account your enterprise establishes with AWS.

# Date, Security, Privacy, and Governance

One of the biggest concerns with enterprise usage of cloud services rendered by a third-party service provider is data integrity. The looming concerns of data integrity impact the degree of trust embedded in third-party service providers who have been found negligent in effectively implementing security control and risk management for customer data hosted in SaaS, IaaS, and PaaS environments. Software as a Service (SaaS) faces the daunting task of information security with data at rest and in transmission via the Internet. Common concerns include service provider personnel and their compliance rates not aligning with federal and state law and policy. Therefore, it is vital to effectively research your service provider and the Service Level Agreements to make sure the services and products relied on are safe and secure. When using Infrastructure as a Service (IaaS), information security is extremely important. After all, there are several technical and security issues that require investigating when relying on a cloud service stack using IaaS. Most issues with IaaS are security concerns, including digital forensics, new attack strategies, resource sharing, and operational trust modes. When dealing with Platform as a Service (PaaS), concerns typically include challenges surrounding cloud stacks, including service life cycle optimization, market and legislative issues, multi-cloud architecture, and adaptive self-preservation. Thus, your enterprise's IT policy must integrate the CIA triad to assure confidentiality, integrity, and availability are woven into business production and operation of services, particularly third-party service sharing.

# Data Privacy

Email privacy is essential. Utilizing a policy that enforces multi-factor authentication log-in access for all personnel is required, and passwords should be changed every 30 days. Doing so helps maintain security and prohibits unauthorized access to system environments. Data privacy for cloud service usage and security requires policy usage for TCP/IP and encryption layer security. This prevents vulnerabilities from developing into economically crippling threats.

# Cloud Vendor Governance Strategy

It is important the cloud policy correlate with the information technology and information security policy. Each policy delivers governance procedures that protect the security of data developed, stored, and transmitted via the enterprise's technology tools. This reinforces personnel's role and responsibilities for protecting the enterprise's information systems and information assets hosted in cloud services. To help improve usage of your enterprise cloud vendor governance strategy, I developed the following outline to provide information on the key components you "must" include in your enterprise's cloud policy:

- **Security awareness and training**

  All personnel must be provided information and guidelines about what must be kept confidential within the daily business operations and physical parameters of the enterprise headquarters. This includes training personnel about integrity and deploying required federal recommendations and guidelines of the CIA triad and the National Institute of Standards and Technology to meet the needs of your enterprise. One policy of great significance is NIST SP 500-291. Furthermore, the National Initative for Cybersecurity Education Workforce Framework under NIST Sp 800-181A is a supporting guideline that explains why training should include an awareness agreement enabling personnel to sign and retain a copy of the consent to engage in security awareness training for their own keeping, while a copy of this document should be inserted in each employee file.

A confidentiality form should also be provided to each personnel being trained. Security training should educate and prepare personnel on their role and responsibilities as well as what is considered a breach of trust, what cloud and physical technology tools must be secured, and how to secure those environments, that is, stacks, Instances, and keypairs as well as software, hardware, computers, mobile devices, Wi-Fi, and Internet access. Employees should be trained to know how to update their passwords and account log-in data in alignment with the enterprise's security requirements, that is, multi-factor authentication. Training should be deployed quarterly. Penalties for violation should encourage compliance. Noncompliance must be reprimanded stringently to enhance the value of policy compliance. All policy should be updated as needed and annually, in alignment with updates deployed by federal and state laws and policy.

- **Incident response and security event plans**

All personnel must be given strict instructions to respond to incidents as they occur. This must include whom to contact, what steps to take when an issue has been discovered, and how to effectively record the issue. Thus, an Incident Response Template should be given to all personnel in their security awareness training package, and personnel should be reminded of the importance of this document. This document should be given to the department manager and the IT manager. Duplicated copies should be stored in the employee's file and the file of any manager who took an active role in overseeing the containment of the issue.

If a security breach has been successful, it is important procedures of assessing the issue are provided and a written record is kept on file. If the event was an external attack, a report should be made relating to all events that occurred during and after the attack was discovered. If necessary, a police report must be filed, that is, if the attack was valued high on the scale of risk factors and needs to be investigated for criminal prosecution. Otherwise, procedures to retain data regarding the incident should align with proper policy protocol.

If the incident occurred within the cloud environment, the same must apply, but the steps to contain the event should include screen captures of the cloud Instance dashboard, including dates and timeline stamps as well as names of all personnel involved. This data should be provided to department managers and remain confidential until a thorough investigation has been conducted. The investigation should include assessing what happened, and support from the vendor should be rendered and effectively provided, with steps of containment if a plan has not been successful prior to the attack.

- **Data handling**

All data stored on file in on-site technology environments and in the virtual cloud must be secured. Data compiled must be kept confidential and made available to those authorized to access the data as needed. All data handling should be "as needed" with strict "confidentiality." Violators of this code of security should be held to strict penalties to avoid future incidence and policy violations. All technology that stores or transmits data should be effectively secured using anti-virus software, intrusion detection and prevention software, encryption, and system backups. This applies to both physical technology and cloud environments. Records are required to be written clearly and convey all required information to assure accuracy and integrity are deployed and infused throughout all daily activities conducted on behalf of the enterprise, both with physical technology tools and virtual cloud environments. Policy should also include procedures for data handling and securing as well as data disposal and data retention. In addition, policy should include access to systems, including account management procedures, acceptable use, software usage, system access, physical security, virtual private cloud security, and vendor compliance.

- **Security technology resources**

There must be email security and accessibility and accountability policy, clean desk and clear screen policy, effective security of all cloud services, encryption policy, mobile device policy, password management, removeable media, social media policy, and wireless communication policy. Policy should also include security procedures for Wi-Fi and Internet access both internally and via the network when working off campus.

# Business and Technical Impact Analysis

Operating on-premises services and virtual business services in the cloud requires you to conduct ongoing risk analysis. The risk analysis should never be avoided! Table 4-2 provides an example of an asset analysis evaluating the risk and the impact of asset risk. You will then assess a business disruption scenario, to give you some idea of how to effectively consider your assets at risk and the impact of those assets at risk and at what cost do the enterprise, stakeholders, and executive board members suffer during a downtime relating to natural catastrophes and power outages. This is important to consider.

***Table 4-2.***

| Assets at Risk | The impact of assets as risk |
|---|---|
| People | Disclosure of sensitive data/unauthorized |
| Physical location, that is, tornado, storms, | access |
| hurricane | Damage/fire/burglary/increased insurance cost |
| Computers | Hacked/system corruption |
| Software applications | Malware |
| Data | Confiscation/stolen/sold on the Dark Web |
| Privacy | Invasion of sensitive data/violating privacy rights |
| Information technology | Data corruption/hardware and software |
| Information systems | corruption |
| Reputation | Loss of clients, customers, and stakeholders |
| Regulations | Fines and legal fees |
| Policy | Loss of revenue/lawsuits |
| Contracts | Replacement cost/time of work lost |
| Equipment/utility outages | |

# Business Disruption Scenario

The physical location of the enterprise could face natural weather conditions, that is, hurricane, tornado, or flooding. This can impact daily operations and decrease revenue earnings during the downtime of physical location operations. There could also be damage and/or breakdown of machinery, that is, fax machines and printers, building card access outages, Internet not connecting, Wi-Fi not connecting, or broadband not connecting. System outages can impact usage of electricity, which halt daily operations and decrease revenue earnings for whatever amount of time. If a storm disrupts the electricity flow within a district because the powerlines have been torn down by the wind, it could be days before the lines are repaired. Thus, if the company relies on the electricity and is making daily revenue of $100,000 and the power lines are down for a week, the company loses $500,000 for that week. Disruption of supply chain efforts includes a lack of delivery for supplies and products to consumers and manufacturers; physical servers could be destroyed and/or confiscated, and computers could be damaged and/or stolen. Printers and fax machines can also be without power to operate.

# Exit Strategy

One of the most invaluable components to partnering with cloud vendors is not only understanding the Service Level Agreement and how that impacts the governance of the partnership but also understanding your legal opportunities to terminate the partnership contract, when necessary, without penalization. Thus, an exit strategy is essential to protecting your enterprise from legal issues that can be costly. In fact, research conveys "The European Network and Information Security Agency (ENISA) and European Commission (EC) have recognized the vendor lock-in problem as one of the greatest obstacles to enterprise cloud adoption" [1]. Further research reports that vendor lock-in can impact technical compatibilities when trying to end a partnership with a cloud vendor. Issues arise regarding interface compatibility, whereas the data storage in one cloud environment may not be conducive when migrating to another cloud vendor. Thus, before contracting with Amazon Web Services, you need to plan an effective "escape route" and explain how it aligns with the AWS Service Level Agreement. Therefore, your exit strategy should include specifics.

For instance, if your enterprise is using Software as a Service (SaaS), Platform as a Service (PaaS), or Infrastructure as a Service (IaaS), research conveys utilizing IaaS as "the repatriation will be easier, even at scale, then if your application has many dependencies on higher level PaaS offerings" [2]. Thus, it is recommended your enterprise makes sure it can relinquish any contract with AWS if needed to avoid legal complications. Furthermore, being prepared to modify current cloud environments that may not be easily adaptable to a new vendor should be considered. So relying on multi-cloud vendor applications to avoid vendor lock-in should also be considered. With multiple geographical locations, this benefits your enterprise greatly. It also helps decrease concerns about service incompatibility. In fact, research explains that open source infrastructure is always the best approach. After all, "open source infrastructure components like Kubernetes or OpenShift cluster or open-source databases can make a move between cloud much easier. The more proprietary services you use, the harder it will be to adapt your application to run in a new cloud environment" [3].

# Evaluation of Cloud Service Offering Architecture Email and Architecture for Email in the Cloud

Email as a Service (EaaS) requirements need to be effective to support your enterprise goal of managing workload requirements for email. Research helps understand the value of assessing AWS based on performance, capacity, cost, and availability requirements. In fact, research conveys "addressing performance-related challenges in SaaS environments starts with producing tenant-aware metrics and insights. These metrics allow you to detect tenant consumption trends, how tenants are experiencing the service, and evaluate how the service is responding to tenant workload variations" [4]. Utilizing EaaS enables effective metrics to be compiled from each tenant; these metrics enable detection of any modification in each tenant's consumption profile as well as enable the development of strategies to accommodate distinct tenant needs and optimize the software's performance efficiency [5].

When there are concerns regarding the capacity of Email as a Service (EaaS) deployed by AWS, Amazon WorkMail enables enterprises to effectively manage corporate email infrastructure. This service enables data at rest to be encrypted, which can be instrumental in decreasing the number of successful cyber-attacks that penetrate the firewall implemented to protect the system. Utilizing AWS services for email will also enable your enterprise to retain full control over data locality by simply electing the AWS geographical region where all data is stored. Furthermore, this service enables your enterprise personnel to continue utilizing their Microsoft Outlook email accounts without having to install or update additional software. In fact, AWS email services will also enable your enterprise's personnel to align their current email accounts with their mobile devices without fear of unauthorized intrusion incidence. Thus, integration with the current Microsoft Active Directory can reduce the stress to align with AWS services. Furthermore, utilizing AWS Email as a service (EaaS) helps reduce cost. This reduction in cost enables your enterprise to maintain its current budget and not worry about having to increase cost based on usage and/or the number of email accounts utilized.

Another benefit is having access to AWS Email as a Service (EaaS), 24/7/365, across all geographical locations your enterprise operates offices in and connecting with their target audience. AWS Email as a Service can be a reliable and trusted tool your enterprise should consider investing in. Relying on AWS EC2 Instances and virtual email within the AWS cloud environment enables your enterprise to effectively utilize a secure virtual email service that meets the long-term needs of the enterprise, for connecting multiple workplace locations. In fact, Figure 4-1 provides a diagram of the AWS EaaS infrastructure, reporting how this service is developed and implemented.

***Figure 4-1.*** *EaaS infrastructure*

The preceding figure conveys multiple geographical locations for four primary offices. The internal building embodies an Internet service rendered by a local service provider, which is accessed through the Wi-Fi installed in each location. These different locations share access to the AWS EaaS across the Wide Access Network and each Local Area Network. There is a consistency of subnetted IP addresses that enables your enterprise to work across multiple geographical locations, with low concern of threat because a virtual private network is relied upon and all geographical locations accessing the Wi-Fi and Internet are encrypted. The AWS EaaS encryption helps reduce threats and unauthorized intrusion of information systems and cloud environments.

# Evaluation of Cloud Service Offering Architecture for Software Development and Architecture Design for Software Development Kit in the Cloud

Relying on an effective Software Development Kit enables an enterprise to optimize its ability to increase brand awareness across all geographical locations while deploying efficient information security management. In fact, Amazon Web Services provides the Cloud Development Kit, which delivers essential tools for popular programming languages, such as Python and Java, as well as reduces the need to install files. AWS Cloud9 provides a seamless opportunity for developing serverless applications that helps your enterprise easily define resources, effectively debug, and alternate between local and remote execution of serverless applications. The AWS Cloud Development Kit is open source and utilizes familiar programming languages and provides "high-level components called constructs that preconfigure cloud resources with proven defaults, so you can build cloud applications without needing to be an expert. AWS CDK provisions your resources in a safe, repeatable manner through AWS Cloud Formation. It also enables you to compose and share your own custom constructs that incorporate your organization's requirements, helping you start new projects faster" [6]. Most importantly, relying on AWS CDK prevents your enterprise from needing to concern about its current integrated development environment (IDE) because the CDK enables your enterprise to create its cloud application without leaving the current IDE. In fact, you can write your runtime code and establish your AWS resources utilizing the same programming language. You can also visualize your CDK application stacks and resources utilizing the AWS Toolkit for VS code [7]. AWS CDK also enables an ease of development by simply downloading pre-configured application components from a package manager or repository.

Additionally, AWS CDK defines the application in a programming language and provisions the application with AWS CloudFormation. Doing so enables your enterprise to effectively manage the overall development and usage of an AWS Software Development Kit and manage the cost associated with such. Furthermore, utilizing AWS CDK will enable your enterprise to effectively interact with your CDK service application and manage synthesizing a CFN template, which conveys the difference among running stacks and any proposed modifications as well as confirms security concerns correlating with upgrades before deploying multiple stacks between multiple locations [8]. Suggested command lines commonly deployed include

- CDK init – This command line conveys the desired template, that is, app, and the type of programming language, that is, Python.

- CDK synth – This command line executes your app and causes the resources defined in it to be translated into an AWS CloudFormation template.

- CDK diff – Embodies four sections, that is, IAM policy and statement changes, parameters, and resources.

- CDK deploy – Displays progress details.

AWS offers end users an ease of clarity in understanding their CDK Explorer. This tool helps you visually assess your enterprise applications, infrastructure stacks, and additional resources and policies. This is a good way to manage usage of your enterprise CDK as well as decrease unauthorized modifications as security vulnerabilities. The following is a diagram of the proposed AWS CDK for BallotOnline, where I utilized a Bash/Python coding language within the AWS Cloud9 environment to achieve the end goal:

Step_1 AWS EC2 Instance-Launch and run

Step_2 Enter AWS Cloud9 Console and code with Python using command line interface

Example: aws [options] <command> <subcommand> [parameters]

Step_3 Bash- "ip-171-21-20-128"

vocstartsoft:~/environment $ aws ec2 create-vpc-cidr-block 10.0.0.0/16

Next, AWS recommends using the following Syntax [9]:

```
JSON
{
"Type": "AWS::EC2:: VPC"'
"Properties": {
"CIDRBLOCK": String,
"EnableDNSHostnames": Boolean,
"EnableDNSSupport":  Boolean,
"InstanceTenancy": String,
"Tags": [Tag,...]
}
}
```

AWS explains each command line interface. The CIDR block relies on the primary IPV4. However, with the decrease in available IP addresses relying on IPv4, you should improve your enterprise ability to align its subnetted IP addresses with IPV6; this enables your enterprise to increase its number of available IP addresses. In fact, "the Internet Protocol version 4 (IPv4) is a protocol for use on packet-switched Link Layer networks (e.g., Ethernet). IPv4 provides an addressing capability of approximately 4.3 billion addresses. The Internet Protocol version 6 (IPv6) is more advanced and has better features compared to IPv4. It has the capability to provide an infinite number of addresses. In fact, it is now replacing IPv4 to accommodate the growing number of networks worldwide and help solve the IP address exhaustion problem" [10].

When deploying the Enable DNS Hostname command line to invoke Instances in the virtual private cloud to acquire DNS or not, the Enable DNS Support command line determines if the DNS resolution is enabled by the VPC or not. After all, DNS is enabled by default. The Instance tenancy enables Instances launched into the VPC to be configured by default or dedicated. Unless the tenancy is configured during the launch, it runs by default. Most importantly, "tags" are simply designated for the VPC.

# Evaluation of Cloud Service Offering Architecture for Backup and Archiving and Architecture Design for Backup and Archiving in the Cloud

Amazon Web Services provides a detailed outline of effective methods to deploy backup and archiving of data within the VPC. Utilizing the Commvault software AWS offers enables your enterprise to back up to the cloud, oversee disaster recovery, and protect workloads running in the cloud. Backup and archiving with AWS can be done "at the primary on-premises location by writing directly to an external cloud provider's storage solution, or retaining a local copy and replicating the backup/archive data (either in full or only selective portions of that data) into an external cloud provider's storage service" [11]. With AWS, you can trust all data stored in the cloud is protected, which minimizes cost. In fact, the billing approach enables you to provision Instances for backup as needed and align the current enterprise backup and archiving or recovery policy with the standards and recommendations of AWS. Moreover, this enables you to begin relying on a cost per disaster recovery event, instead of paying for availability. This will improve your enterprise level of disaster recovery preparedness within the application. This also enables your enterprise to access unlimited resources to both design disaster recovery tests and execute disaster recovery events, to assess any vulnerabilities that may be present within the VPC. This can be achieved without purchasing additional hardware or impacting daily operations [12].

With AWS Commvault client-side de-duplication, your enterprise can reduce backup window and increase scale, which helps free up bandwidth for production and backup network traffic [13]. Furthermore, the Commvault software delivers crash and application consistent backups that provide flexibility as well as storage-level replication. This enables your enterprise to utilize object storage layer between regions. "However, in the circumstance that bad or corrupted blocks are replicated to the secondary region, your recovery points are invalid. While Commvault software can support a Replicated Cloud Library model, AWS recommends configuring Commvault software to create an independent copy of your data, whether to another region or cloud provider to address that risk. De-duplication is also vital as part of this process, as it means that Commvault software can minimize the cross-region/cross-provider copy by ensuring only the unique changed blocks are transferred over the wire" [14].

In addition, utilizing the Commvault software enables your enterprise to trust in automation of software deployment delivered through three components, that is, programmatic data management, workload auto-detection and auto-protection, and self-service access and restore. With programmatic data management, the Commvault software enables you to access and control the robust application interface, including deployment, configuration, backup, and restore points within the solution (2021). Furthermore, the workload auto-detection and auto-protection enable you to rest assured the automated application relinquishes the need for someone to manually update the software to protect elected created datasets. Instead, the software automatically enables improved resiliency within the cloud environment to ensure all data is protected and any recovery points are effectively managed (2021). The last important point to remember is that the Commvault software enables your enterprise to rely on the self-service interface to access its datasets via a web-based interface that enables security within individual files and folders in protected datasets. Doing so frees up personnel to focus on critical tasks (2021). Figure 4-2 demonstrates an architecture representing backup and archiving in the cloud.

***Figure 4-2.*** *Backup and archiving configuration*

Figure 4-2 conveys the transition of the current on-premises storage environment within BallotOnline headquarters that is being uploaded to the virtual private cloud EC2 Instance. Utilizing three additional backup and archiving environments offered by the same service provider or others provides an assurance that data is backed up and archived effectively. There is also a need for integration of Secure Sockets Layer (SSL) and encryption that should be applied to backup and archiving on all web-based interface environments connecting to the virtual private network (VPN). All data must be encrypted and password protected utilizing a keypair to limit authorized access to only the chief cloud engineer and selected authorized personnel.

# Cloud Monitoring Solution for Backup and Archiving

Amazon CloudWatch delivers effective services that capture the metrics and provide statistics regarding the consumption for backup and archiving. AWS provides information to help enterprises comprehend namespaces, metrics, dimensions, resolution, statistics, percentiles, and alarms needed to manage CloudWatch services. This service helps determine the amount of storage needed to effectively conduct backup and archiving. After all, metrics "represents a time-ordered set of data points that are published to Cloud Watch" [15]. Moreover, metrics are considered variables to monitor, while data points represent the value of those variables, that is, metrics, over a period. Since your enterprise will be relying on AWS EC2 Instances, metrics are rendered as default without cost. However, your enterprise can pay a fee for services that include detailed monitoring, specifically for the EC2 Instance relied on. Fees typically include an established set fee that your enterprise elects. And if your enterprise has offices across different geographical locations, paying cost for backup and archiving is essential. After all, metrics can only exist in the region they are created in.

In addition, CloudWatch enables your enterprise to ingest complex high-cardinality application data with logs and create actionable metrics for those logs. This will enable your enterprise to embed custom metrics in alignment with those detailed logs that capture event data, and CloudWatch automatically extracts the detailed log metric so your enterprise can visualize as well as set alarms to access and capture real-time incident detection. These detailed log metrics also enable your enterprise to gain clarity regarding the origin of operational events.

For instance, capacity consumption billing information includes monitoring cost and metrics. Thus, your enterprise can simply set its own service usage quotas to visualize service usage through graphs and dashboards. Your enterprise can also set alarms to evaluate when service usage is reaching its set data points. So, when your enterprise enables monitoring of estimated charges for its AWS account, "the estimated charges are calculated and sent several times daily to Cloud Watch as metric data. Billing metric data is stored in the U.S. East (N. Virginia) Region and reflects worldwide charges. This data includes the estimated charges for every service in AWS, you use as well as the estimated overall total of your AWS charges. You can choose to receive alerts by email when charges have exceeded a certain threshold" [16]. Billing alerts can be set by simply configuring the system to compile such. Once this service is configured, it takes 15 minutes to begin compiling billing data and set billing alarms.

# Limitations

Limitations engulfing AWS WorkMail include messages regarding connection loss, secure connection failed, session expired, or mail cannot be saved. Connection loss often encompasses server error messages that may surface when data cannot be retrieved from the server. End users can still utilize the service even though the connection may be loss. In fact, AWS explains that once connection has been reestablished, the warning message is omitted, and end users can continue working. If there is a secure connection message regarding a failed attempt during log-on, AWS recommends updating the web browser to the current browser edition. There are also limitations on the number of emails that can be sent. By default, AWS regulates the number of email messages that can be sent at one time. However, your enterprise can modify this restriction by completing a form that AWS offers to help customers increase the number of emails they can send. However, keep in mind when email is not properly sent, an error message is displayed on the screen. It is recommended to resave the email. With the Commvault software, limitations include canary runtime upgrade and downgrade issues and issues with waiting for elements to appear. There is also concern of nodes being visible or not on HTML elements for page click. Furthermore, there are issues regarding the inability to upload artifacts to S3 Exception as well as the inability to fetch S3 bucket locations. Additional issues include protocol errors, that is, Runtime.callFunction, as well as issues regarding accessing an internal endpoint and troubleshooting a canary on a VPC.

There are limits to the number of vCPUs, which impact operating one or more on-demand Instances within an AWS account. Amazon EC2 measures usage toward each limit based on the total number of vCPUs (virtual Central Processing Units) assigned to the running on-demand Instances in a consumer's AWS account (2021). Additionally, limitations for an AWS on-demand Instance account are set per region. However, limits will change over time. In fact, Amazon EC2 consistently monitors client usage within each region, and the limits are increased automatically based on the use of a given EC2. Most important is security. After all, ineffective security impedes on the ability to effectively store data without concern of tampering and/or unauthorized access or retrieval. Another thing to consider is issues with the CloudWatch agent not launching on start. Troubleshooting should be executed in alignment with AWS recommendations on how to correct these issues.

# Cloud Service Offering for Backups and Archiving

Thus, it is important to consider usage of AWS S3 and AWS Glacier for backup and archiving services for your enterprise legacy system. Doing so not only will cut cost but help increase layers of security. Both S3 and Glacier enable an extensive reliance on API operations and a Software Development Kit that makes integration of these services into legacy on-premises and/or within newly upgraded systems easy to rely on for backup and recovery. Any current backup and archiving and recovery your enterprise is using must align with AWS and its API operations, because AWS backup software is AWS-aware and automatically can back up from on-premises servers and align with AWS S3 and Glacier. With the usage of Amazon Web Services Storage Gateway, your enterprise on-premises system can become scalable within cloud storage. The cloud system supports standard storage efforts that collaborate with your enterprise existing applications as well as enable effective security of all data sources. Furthermore, your enterprise can utilize Storage Gateway as a component for its on-premises block-based storage workloads (2021). Storage Gateway is useful for hybrid situations, which enables an ease of transitioning to the cloud storage for all backups. This can be done either as a VM (virtual machine) or as a dedicated hardware application.

In addition, AWS utilizes File Gateway to deliver a block-based storage for AWS S3 to assure durable offsite backups. This is useful for situations if there is ever a chance to quickly back up recently backed-up files. Because File Gateway enables the SMN and NFS protocols, your enterprise is able to access its files as it has done so when accessing network file share. Your enterprise also can take advantage of AWS S3 object versioning capabilities. Object versioning enables your enterprise the ability to restore previous object versions for a file and easily access such, utilizing SMB or NFS.

# AWS Virtual Private Cloud

Amazon Web Services virtual private cloud has become the most utilized and trusted cloud service provider for millions of corporations and government entities who rely on cloud infrastructure. AWS VPC offers exceptional scalability, reduces cost on budget spending, increases security layers with the integration of encryption on all Application Programming Interfaces, and can be managed by a select few personnel who can access their corporation's sensitive data in compliance with enterprise policy. This is commonly done with reliance on keypairs that are designated during the development of virtual private cloud Instances. Relying on AWS VPC helps your enterprise decrease concerns of security risk and reduce the cost of usage. The VPC can be developed for access by anyone from any geographical location and comes with an encryption system that prevents data leakage as well as modification of data during transit and/or while data is at rest. Key components to concern with within AWS VPC include the subnet, route table, Internet gateways, VPC endpoint, and CIDR block. Because BallotOnline utilizes various regional locations for their offices, BallotOnline needed to subnet IP addresses to assure there were enough IP addresses to support the number of personnel and to increase security of the primary IP address. Additionally, there are concerns regarding the route or rules that govern where network traffic is directed. The VPC helps with transitioning of communication between resources, the Internet, and the

VPC. The VPC endpoint enables your enterprise to privately connect to its VPC services supported by AWS and the VPC endpoint, which are powered by a private link. This connection is done without needing an Internet gateway, NAT device, VPN connection, or AWS direct connection. Furthermore, the VPC does not require public IP addresses to communicate with resources utilized by your enterprise with authorization. Thus, any traffic exchanged between the enterprise VPC and other services will not leave the Amazon network without permission or authorization.

During configuration of the VPC, the software developer develops Instances, which are virtual private clouds hosted within the Software as a Service (SaaS), Platform as a Service (PaaS), or IaaS (Infrastructure as a Service). To do so, steps include accessing the AWS console (`https://console.aws.amazon.com/vpc/`) and creating an Instance name and VPC ID column. This helps identify all components associated with the account. Next, navigating the pane and electing a subnet enables the creation of subnets by name. Furthermore, it is required to navigate the pane to create an Internet gateway, which is attached to the VPC, which requires choosing a route table, that is, two main columns, where the main column displays No and invokes the enterprise to elect the route table to display the route data. Next is deploying the VPC EC2 Instance, which can be done by navigating the AWS EC2 console and creating a name, electing an Instance type, configuring the Instance details, adding tags, configuring a security group, and reviewing everything to make sure all data is input correctly and launched effectively. Doing so enables a smooth transition of services from legacy to virtual private cloud.

# Virtual Private Network (VPN)

Utilizing AWS virtual private network helps establish secure connectivity between your enterprise on-premises networks, remote offices, client devices, and an additional AWS global network. AWS delivers VPN in two service packages: site-to-site VPN, which creates encrypted channels between your enterprise network and its VPC cloud services, and AWS client VPN, which connects to AWS or on-premises resources utilizing a VPN software client. Both services provide highly available, easily managed, elastic cloud VPN solutions that protect an enterprise's network traffic. Because your enterprise may be operating across different geographical locations, the AWS site-to-site VPN helps globally distribute application route network traffic safely to the nearest AWS endpoint, rendering the best performance. Benefits include tunnel redundancy with the usage of two separate tunnels for funneling traffic. There is also an increase of information security with the usage of AWS Global Accelerator. One benefit is robust monitoring. This application works with use cases and can be migrated to work with an enterprise's firewall as well as work between all enterprise's remote sites.

For instance, cost for usage is totaled using this approach: Your enterprise is charged hourly for a site-to-site VPN connection, and the rate is $0.05. The connection is active for 30 days, for 24 hours, with 1,000 GB transferrable in and 500 GB transferrable out. The first GB of data transferred is without cost. However, your enterprise will be charged 499 GB at $0.09 per GB. Thus, the final charge is $44.91 (2021).

During configuration and deployment, it is essential to understand a few terms that play a pivotal role in managing this VPN, such as VPN connection, which establishes a secure connection between on-premises equipment and an enterprise's VPC, and VPN tunnel, which provides an encrypted link to enable data to transfer from a customer network to your enterprise; this is a two-way tunnel that secures all data in transit. A customer gateway provides information to your enterprise and its gateway connections. A customer gateway device is either a physical device or software application on the site-to-site VPN connection. Next, the virtual private gateway enables your enterprise access to a private gateway or transit gateway for AWS site-to-site connection. The transit gateway is a transit hub that interconnects your enterprise and its on-premises networks. The transit gateway can be utilized as the gateway for AWS site-to-site VPN. Limitations to be aware of up front include concerns regarding IPV6 traffic not supported for VPN connections on a virtual private gateway as well as AWS VPN connections not supporting Path MTU Discovery. It is also recommended that when connecting an enterprise's VPN to a common on-premises network, utilizing nonoverlapping CIDR blocks is beneficial. The site-to-site VPN enables reliance on CloudWatch metrics and increases encryption options, such as AES 256-bit encryption, SHA-2 hashing, and additional Diffie-Hellman groups. AWS also enables a private certificate from a subordinate CA from AWS Private Certificate Authority. You can learn more about this at the following link: (`https://docs.aws.amazon.com/vpn/latest/s2svpn/s2s-vpn-user-guide.pdf#VPC_VPN`) (2021).

# AWS S3 Bucket

To store data securely within the infrastructure of AWS S3 requires a bucket. A bucket is a container for objects. Objects are files and metadata describing the file [17]. To store an object in Amazon S3, you must create a bucket and upload the object into that bucket. Once the object is placed in the bucket, you can open it, download it, and transfer it to wherever. Once the stored object or bucket is no longer needed, you can easily clean up its resources. Buckets can contain photos, videos, documents, etc. Once a bucket is created in any AWS region, unlimited objects can be added. Both buckets and objects are AWS resources, and AWS S3 provides APIs to help your enterprise manage those resources.

The configuration of a bucket is a step-by-step process that relies on navigating the AWS console and simply clicking a few tabs and designating titles and creating the environment. Once the namespace is claimed, it cannot be duplicated anywhere else worldwide. Access control lists or bucket policies provide public access to buckets and objects (2021). In fact, your enterprise can configure the application to block public access by modifying the settings to individual buckets or to all buckets within your enterprise account. To assure that all accounts managed by your enterprise under the Amazon S3 buckets and objects, AWS recommends, turning on all four settings for Block Public Access. Doing so prevents public access for all current and future buckets. Configurations can accommodate various needs.

For instance, you can configure your enterprise bucket for website hosting, add a configuration to manage the life cycle of objects in the bucket, and configure the bucket to log access to the bucket. Amazon S3 also supports sub-resources for your enterprise to store and manage the bucket configuration data. There is also object-level configuration, which is considered a sub-resource. Bucket naming has standard rules, for example, names must be between 3 and 63 characters long and names cannot consist only of lowercase letters, numbers, dots, and hyphens. Names must begin and end with a letter or number, and names must not be formatted as an IP address. Names must not start with the prefix xn- as well as not end with the suffix -s3alias.

Once your enterprise creates a bucket, it owns it. Immediately, uploading of objects to the bucket can begin. By default, your enterprise can create up to 100 buckets in each of its accounts. If more buckets are needed, your enterprise can increase the account bucket limit to a maximum of 1,000 buckets by submitting a service limit increase to AWS. However, when relying on the AWS SDK to create a bucket, you must create a client and utilize the client to send request to create a bucket. You can always view the properties enveloped in the S3 bucket by configuring the settings for versioning, tags, default encryption, logging, notifications, and much more. Accessing and making modification requires no coding experience, and because buckets can be accessed using path-style and virtual hosted-style URLs, AWS recommends creating buckets with DNS-compliant bucket names. Amazon Web Services offers an extensive guide for all steps and procedures that must be deployed to effectively manage and maintain an AWS S3 bucket.

# Cloud Synchronization Services

"The NetApp Cloud Sync service offers a simple, secure, and automated way to migrate your data to any target, in the cloud or on your premises. Whether it's a file-based NAS dataset (NFS or SMB), Amazon Simple Storage Service (S3) object format, a NetApp StorageGRID® appliance, or any other cloud provider object store. Cloud Sync can convert and move it for you" [18]. A Software as a Service (SaaS) consisting of a data broker is a cloud-based interface that is available through Cloud Manager and a source and target. Typically, the NetApp data broker software syncs data from any source to a target, which is called a sync relationship. Your enterprise can run the data broker in its AWS cloud infrastructure as well as on-premises. The data broker needs an outbound Internet connection over port 443 to communicate with the Cloud Sync service and contract additional services and repositories. Cost comes in two forms: resource charges and service charges. Resource charges are related to the compute and storage costs for running the data broker in the cloud. There are two ways to pay for sync relationships after the initial 14-day free trial ends. The first option is to subscribe with AWS, to enable your enterprise to pay hourly or annually. Or your enterprise can purchase licenses directly from NetApp.

Furthermore, configuration and deployment requirements must align with AWS S3. For instance, bucket requirements include supporting data broker locations for AWS S3 sync relations that encompass S3 storage as well as a data broker deployed in AWS or on-premises. Also, permissions included in a JSON file must be applied to the S3 bucket so the data broker can access it. Please be advised that your enterprise's local web browser requires access to endpoints for certain actions. Thus, if your enterprise needs to limit outbound connectivity, it is recommended it refer to standard endpoints when configuring a firewall for outbound traffic. Configuration and deployment for data broker software in alignment with AWS requires electing the AWS data broker option to deploy the data broker software on a new EC2 Instance in a VPC. Once Cloud Sync deploys the data broker in AWS, it will create a security group that enables the required outbound communication to exist. However, it is important to understand that NetApp recommends configuring the source, target, and data broker to utilize a Network Time Protocol (NTP) service. Moreover, the time difference between the three components should not exceed 5 minutes.

Configuration and deployment of the Cloud Sync service includes establishing a sync relationship. This helps create the Cloud Sync service copy files from the source to the target. Once the initial copy is made, the service syncs any changed data every 24 hours. Cost can be met two ways, subscribing from AWS to pay as you go or annually, or your enterprise can purchase licenses directly from NetApp.

# Data Backups and Archiving to Cloud Using Cloud Sync Services

One effective method of data backup and archiving to cloud is relying on cloud sync services. NetApp Cloud Backup offers service for cloud volumes and on-premises ONTAP clusters that deliver efficient and secure backup and restore capabilities for protection as well as for long-term archiving. The benefits include ten times faster backup in under 2 minutes time with just a simple click. For example, anyone can simply click for on-premises or cloud volume, activate the retention policy for the selected volume, and be done. S3 is a supported SaaS, IaaS, and PaaS and can reduce concerns regarding encryption, reliability, cost effectiveness, backup cost retention, as well as instant granular data recovery. Use cases commonly include cloud backup and archiving, disaster recovery, ransomware protection, and modernization. Pricing ranges from pay-as-you-go starting at $0.05 GB per month, 12-month subscription at $0.0475 per GB monthly, or 36-month subscription at $0.0425 per GB monthly.

# AWS Service Catalog

AWS Service Catalog is an administrative guide that helps educate administrators and end users of the tools, technology, and support readily available to support the needs of the enterprise during its upgrade and installation of technology tools and APIs as well as during its continued reliance on AWS EC2 Instance and VPC. AWS Service Catalog enables you to create and manage a catalog of IT services AWS approves to be utilized. Such IT services include virtual machine images, servers, software, databases, and in some instances multi-tier application architectures. This service catalog helps you effectively manage commonly deployed IT services as well as helps you achieve consistent management and align business operations with compliance requirements. In addition, this service catalog enables end users to quickly deploy only approved IT services an enterprise elects and approves and invokes an alignment and consistency of constraints enacted by the enterprise.

The configuration and deployment of AWS Service Catalog includes registering an AWS account, which can be accessed via `https://portal.aws.amazon.com/billing/signup`. Once an account has been established, it is important to follow all instructions to gain access to AWS Management Console. Next, granting permission to whomever will need access to the AWS Identity and Access Management is important. Permission must also be granted to service catalog administrators and service catalog end users. Administrators have the responsibility of effectively creating and managing products, adding template constraints, adding launch constraints, and enabling end users access to elected and approved products. Policies must be attached to all IAM users and groups. Granting permission usually includes accessing the IAM console and configuring an elected user. Then programmatic access is granted via AWS Management Console. Permissions are selected, and all existing policies must be attached. If policy is not created, it can be easily created and named.

The same is applied to end users. However, in the IAM console, administrators create a group and can name that group, that is, end users. Once the group is established, policies are created and attached, as well as permissions. The next important step includes downloading the AWS CloudFormation template, which describes the resources your enterprise desires to provision. The template is also useful in declaring resources that should be created when the product is launched. Then a keypair must be created to help secure the product elected for provision, and an AWS Service Catalog portfolio must be created.

The next step includes creating an AWS Service Catalog of products and then adding a template constraint to limit Instance and adding a launch constraint to assign an IAM role. Furthermore, you must grant end users access to the portfolio before testing the end users' experience. Template resources include AWS template format version, parameters, metadata, mappings, resources, as well as provided outputs. One important element of the AWS Service Catalog template is security for the cloud and security in the cloud.

# Cloud Operations End User Guide

It is imperative to develop, implement, and manage effective end user guides on cloud operations. Instructions should convey clearly written methods, procedures, and strategies for each personnel being assessed and trained to impact the comprehension of each participant to align their actions with the role and responsibilities designated for that actor. When the training material is not developed clearly and does not provide information that is relevant to current trends in the subject matter, it impacts the ability to effectively communicate to each personnel the right instructions and policy they should align their actions with. In addition, the end user guide must align with the AWS Service Catalog end user console. Accessing AWS Management Console and accessing

AWS Service Catalog can be done by clicking this link: `https://console.aws.amazon.com/servicecatalog/`. Furthermore, it is essential to have knowledge on the usability of AWS Service Catalog. Doing so enables the enterprise to align all daily operations with the recommendations of AWS services and utilize effective training and education material to increase usage and sharing of the knowledge attained.

# Cloud Operations Administration Guide

Effectively aligning all administrative guidelines for cloud operations should include gaining knowledge of the laws, regulations, and policy governing administrative guidelines for cloud operations. AWS provides a clearly conveyed administrative guide for cloud operations that can enable an enterprise to integrate its current information system with the cloud Platform as a Service (PaaS) rendered by AWS EC2 Instance and VPC services. Aligning all training material with the regulations and standards required to increase productivity of the knowledge learned is important to learning the results of the assessment conducted on each end user. AN AWS service includes a guideline that helps effectively manage cloud operations administratively. This guideline can be accessed via the AWS website. The information security requirements are clearly conveyed and provide a strategy to achieve the results sought.

# Configuration and Deployment of AWS Service Catalog

Your enterprise can utilize the AWS Service Catalog console to examine a list of products and provisioned products that are available to support the enterprise business needs. In fact, you can launch products, view, update, and delete provisioned products your enterprise launches. AWS works diligently to provide the support your enterprise may need during the life cycle of the enterprise and the usage of services provided by AWS. In addition, you must create two IAM users with baseline permissions in each account to effectively establish AWS Service Catalog. Deploying this will support any AWS S3 bucket product in the portfolio.

Additionally, you can select utilize templates provided by AWS to elect the Amazon S3 Bucket AWS CloudFormation templates you create. You can also create constraint types to launch products your enterprise creates. However, "the AWS configuration design requires each AWS Service Catalog product to have either a launch constraint or a stack set constraint. Failure to follow this step could result in an Unable to Retrieve Parameter error in the Service Now Service Catalog" (2021).

Finally, your enterprise is given the ability to establish its Platform as a Service (PaaS) and operate a secure information database that collects analysis and convey statistics that benefit the research of the enterprise, during all development and usage of cloud Platform as a Service (PaaS). AWS Service Catalog also enables you to centrally manage commonly deployed IT services as well as enables you to achieve consistent governance and meet compliance requirements. Utilizing AWS Service Catalog embodies benefits, including standardization. Additional benefits include self-service discovery and launch, fine-grained access control, and extensibility and version control.

## Limitations

Utilizing AWS Service Catalog to increase employee compliance and alignment with roles and responsibilities helps your enterprise effectively deploy a strategy to manage the cloud operations launched in the AWS EC 2 Instance and with the VPC. However, it is essential to comprehend the responsibilities your enterprise will inherit from partnering with AWS services. Neglecting to do so can result in penalties, that is, financial or otherwise, that can impact the reputation of the enterprise. Thus, the enterprise must remain compliant with the regulations and guidelines rendered by AWS to support the usage of all AWS services. Neglecting to effectively assess the enterprise's personnel responsible for managing the cloud operations and information assets and systems to determine their comprehension level of the learning instruction provided impacts understanding the needs of personnel to enable them to align their lives with their commitment to the enterprise.

## Summary

Effective implementation of cloud security policy is a vital step to deter unauthorized access to the enterprise's virtual private cloud. In fact, policy must align with the National Institute of Standards and Technology recommendations and guidelines to increase compliance and improve the rate of successful deterrence efforts that thwart unwanted attacks and unauthorized intrusion. Policy must be developed to include all branches of information technology, information systems, and virtual private cloud infrastructure, to govern those responsible for developing, implementing, and managing the enterprise's information assets. Therefore, deploying a strategic policy scope that aligns cloud usage with existing IT policy is important. However, be sure to utilize the Growth Projection Analysis to help control budget spending cost, and stay current with Service Level Agreements. It is also important to continue managing an effective communication model that helps protect the enterprise from liabilities and increased penalties for noncompliance. Working with multiple service providers can be helpful, but AWS works to meet the needs of your enterprise to increase trust and information security assurance. The business and technical impact analysis will be useful in helping assess the risk and the impact that risk can have on the enterprise and its information assets and technology tools. Most importantly, stay knowledgeable of the trends in cloud service offering architecture for software development and architecture design for Software Development Kits in the cloud. One last thing, when you install a backup and recovery plan that works to control security vulnerabilities, the chance of successful cloud attacks decreases by 80%. So, in the next chapter, you will be reintroduced to the total cost of ownership analysis and increase knowledge awareness about effective disaster recovery and backup for cloud service usage. You will also learn how to effectively implement information technology service planning and gain instrumental clarity regarding the value of a return-on-investment analysis.

# Discussion Questions

1. Why should you develop a Growth Projection Analysis?

2. Why are Service Level Agreements in the cloud important?

3. Cloud vendor governance strategies should include what key components?

4. How do business and technical issues align with the exit strategy?

5. How beneficial are cloud monitoring solutions for backup and archiving?

6. Why should your enterprise rely on AWS virtual private cloud?

7.  What is a virtual private network?

8.  What benefits does AWS S3 bucket provide?

9.  Why should you rely on cloud synchronization services?

10. What is the purpose of AWS Service Catalog?

# CHAPTER 5

# Cloud Orchestration and Automation

**Learning Objectives**

> Understand the total cost of ownership analysis.
>
> Understand how to effectively deploy disaster recovery and backup for cloud service usage.
>
> Understand how to effectively implement information technology service planning.
>
> Understand the value of a return-on-investment Analysis.

Throughout this book, you gained information regarding the steps, methods, and strategies utilized to support the enterprise goals of BallotOnline and their decision to migrate their usage of an on-premises information system and networking to the virtual private cloud infrastructure delivered through AWS. You also learned about the struggles and challenges BallotOnline endured to achieve their business goals. Furthermore, you learned the value of assessing the needs of the enterprise and its cloud usage architecture as well as learned the importance of planning, developing, implementing, and effectively managing cloud orchestration and automation. In this last chapter, you will gain understanding of some use case service management tools AWS renders. Current use cases provided by Amazon Web Services include data analytics, operational intelligence, variable analytic workloads, software test automation, configuration management, monitoring for containers, Internet of Things, device operation management, monitoring and response automation, remote management and monitoring, predictive maintenance, transit VPC, infrastructure software, backup and recovery, web application firewall, intrusion detection, business continuity, application monitoring, machine learning use cases, data science tools, migration, integrating with SAP, cloud workload security, endpoint detection, as well as security use cases.

© Bradley Fowler 2023
B. Fowler, *AWS for Public and Private Sectors*, https://doi.org/10.1007/978-1-4842-9048-4_5

Each use case has monthly cost, which requires individual assessments of cost for services your enterprise plans to utilize. Thus, it is important to understand how to assess the cost of services for your enterprise. One way to help you understand is recommending usage of the AWS Pricing Calculator. This key component helps you plan for the services needed and assess how to effectively manage cost reduction. Therefore, you will be reintroduced to the total cost of ownership analysis as well as gain understanding about the value of a return-on-investment analysis. The total cost of ownership delivers a management assessment tool that helps justify the enterprise investments and can help align the enterprise's IT operations efficiency goals with the enterprise business performance requirements. After all, TCO for cloud computing reduces cost than comparable with on-premises operations; however, business maturity level should also be considered. In fact, you should keep in mind that TCO focuses primarily on the direct and indirect cost, while return-on-investment analysis focuses on costs vs. the benefits of your enterprise cloud investment.

# Cloud Service Catalog Overview

Amazon Service Catalog enables your enterprise to develop and manage catalogs for IT services the enterprise acquires through its partnership with AWS. Such services include virtual machine images, servers, software, and databases that support multi-tier application architecture. Furthermore, AWS Service Catalog enables your enterprise to effectively manage deployed information technology services and all applications, resources, and metadata. Doing so enables your enterprise to achieve consistent management and remain compliant as well as align policy with federal and state compliance requirements. AWS Service Catalog will also enable effective management of costs, performance, security, compliance, and operational status for application levels. Benefits commonly include regulations compliance standards.

For instance, your enterprise can control which IT services and versions are readily available and determine what is configured for each available service as well as determine who can have access permission by individual, group, or department. Your enterprise can also control usage of IT services by designating constraints, including limiting AWS regions, and which products can be launched. In fact, Figure 5-1 provides a sample of an initial workflow for an administrator to create a service catalog from AWS.

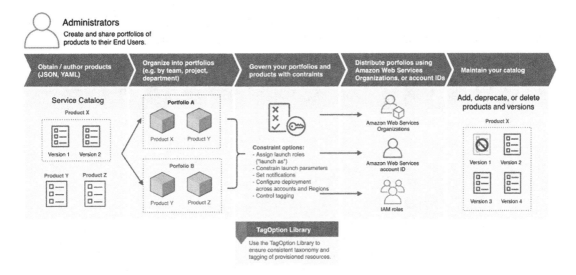

**Figure 5-1.** *Initial workflow for an administrator. Source: Google.com/images.* *(2022). AWS Service Catalog. Retrieved from* `https://bit.ly/3xIfCy4`

Figure 5-1 represents how your enterprise will be able to obtain and develop products using JSON and YAML as well as organize such products into portfolios. This includes effective management of your enterprise portfolios and constraints. Utilizing AWS Service Catalog will enable improved distribution of products using AWS organizations and account IDs. Most importantly, AWS Service Catalog will enable better catalog management.

# Monthly Cost Analysis

The monthly estimated cost analysis provided by Amazon Web Services is an easy-to-use online tool that helps you estimate monthly cost of AWS services based on your expected usage. The AWS Simple Monthly Calculator is always updated with the highest pricing for all AWS services in all regions [1]. However, keep in mind that AWS service pricing varies between different AWS regions. AWS EC2 Instances provide a wide scope of Instance types that render a combination of CPU, memory, storage, I/O, and networking capabilities. Therefore, your enterprise will be charged by the hour for each running instance. Amazon EC2 enables multiple purchasing options, which helps make things flexible and optimize cost. Utilizing on-demand options, your enterprise pays for compute capacity by the hour, absent long-term commitments or up-front payments. This will also enable your enterprise to increase or decrease its compute capacity depending on demands of the applications and only pay specified hourly rates for the Instances utilized. A good example can be viewed in Figures 5-2 and 5-3, reporting the cost of website hosting services per month for BallotOnline.

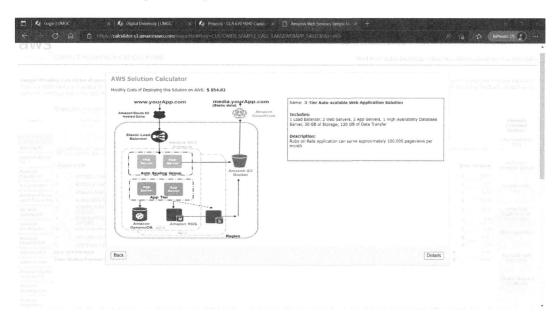

***Figure 5-2.***  *AWS Solution Calculator*

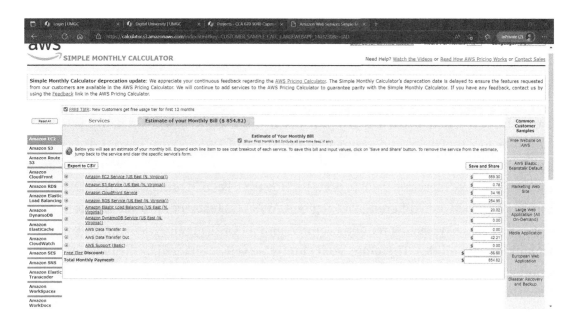

***Figure 5-3.***  *AWS Simple Monthly calculator*

The estimated cost for monthly billing for website hosting is $854.82. Because it is recommended that BallotOnline mirror all services to increase security and decrease possible downtime of services, the estimated cost must be doubled, bringing the estimated monthly cost to $1,709.64. When you assess the estimated cost for your enterprise, you will be able to have a clearer understanding on what the cost for services will be. Another example is provided in Figure 5-4, which reports monthly estimated cost for messaging services rendered by AWS for BallotOnline, which totaled $1,098.00.

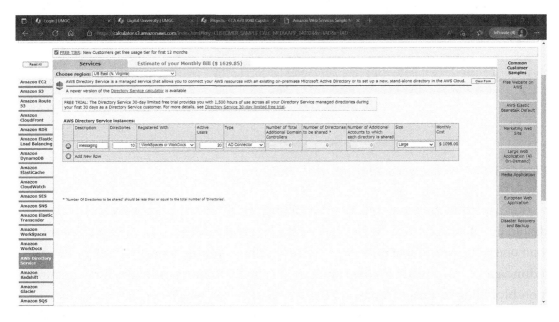

***Figure 5-4.*** *AWS region selection*

This estimate includes cost for 20 active users, registered with WorkSpaces or WorkDocs. This includes ten directories with a large size. The estimate monthly billing cost includes Amazon S3 services at $6.91, Amazon CloudFront service at $505.46, AWS Directory Service at $1098.00; AWS Business Support at $148.17, and an AWS free tier discount of $–128.78, bringing the total cost to $1629.85. Figure 5-5 provides an example of how the calculator lets you input your figures.

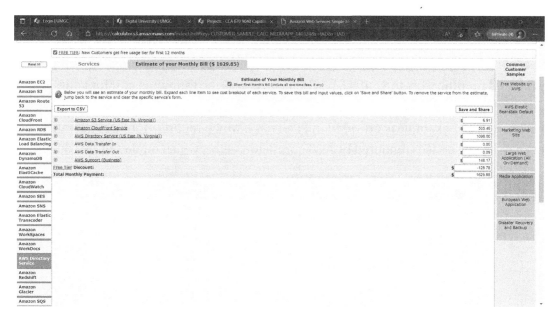

**Figure 5-5.**  *Estimated cost for monthly billing*

Keep in mind the estimated monthly billing cost for disaster recovery and backup should be calculated twice. In fact, having backup and recovery processes with more than one cloud provider at once, you hedge your bets. You're basically adding a layer of redundancy to an already resilient system [2]. Figure 5-6 shows estimates for configuring monthly billing cost using Amazon CloudWatch services, which are configured for disaster recovery and backup. Thus, the custom metric for BallotOnline was configured for ten AWS resources. You will set the custom metric resource for your enterprise differently. But for BallotOnline, the custom metric is set at 12. The frequency of metric data is configured at 5-minute intervals. The alarm type is set to standard with three alarms for each resource, and the ingested log size is set at 15 GB. The archive log size is set at 15 GB, and the vended log size is also set at 15 GB. Next, the log delivered to S3 data ingested is set at 15 GB. Figures 5-6 and 5-7 show the system output for monthly cost at $1334.57. However, this estimate should be calculated twice the amount if your enterprise is deploying multiple disaster recovery and backup plans.

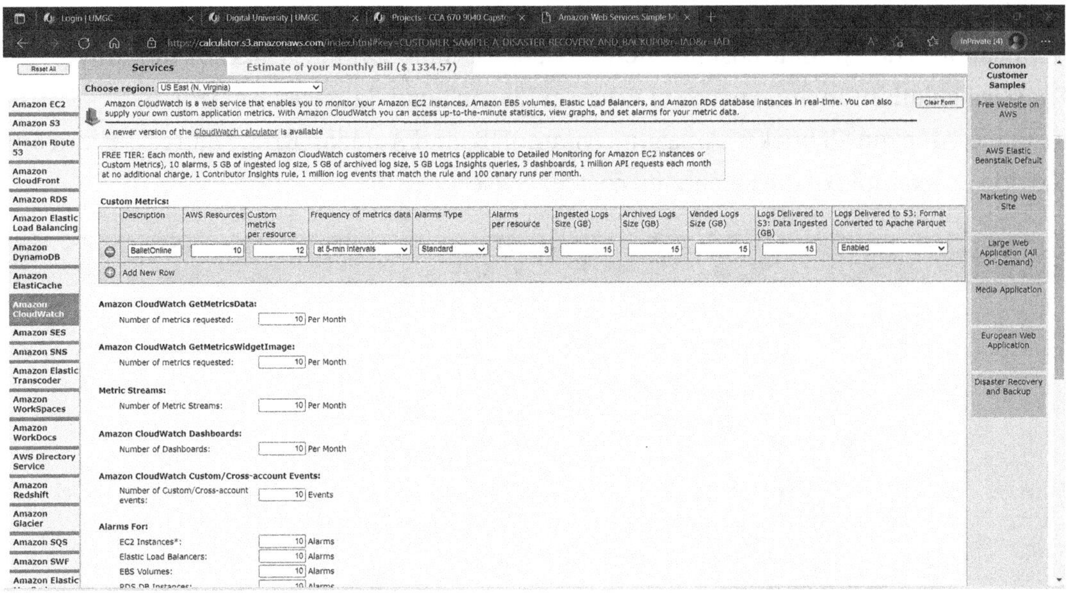

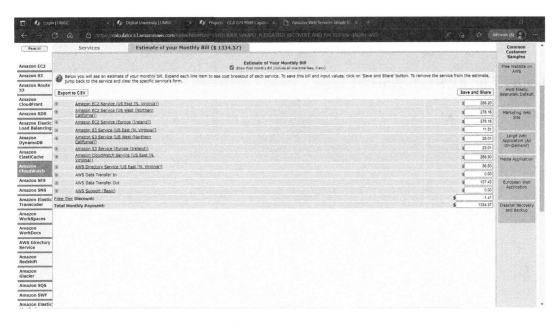

**Figure 5-6.**  *Custom metric selection*

**Figure 5-7.**  *Estimated monthly billing*

Next, you will need to calculate IT self-service, which is classified as Large Web Application. The estimate cost for such services for BallotOnline is $854.82 monthly. These calculations include usage of Amazon Elastic Load Balancer, Amazon EC2 Instance, Amazon S3 bucket, Amazon DynamoDB, and Amazon RDS. Figures 5-8 and 5-9 provide an example of the calculated cost for these services.

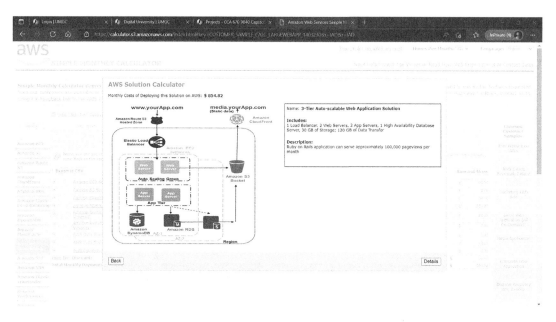

***Figure 5-8.***  *AWS Solution Calculator*

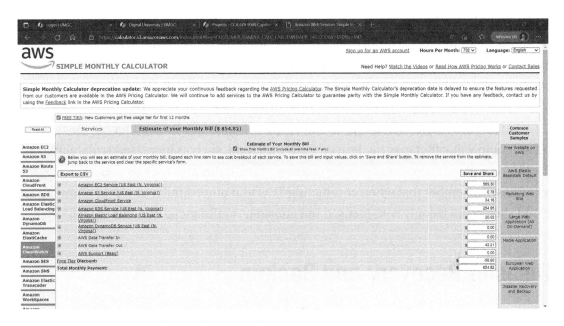

**Figure 5-9.** *Estimated cost for monthly services*

Having knowledge of each tool your enterprise will rely on and the cost for usage per month can enable your enterprise to better manage its monthly budget and decrease usage of services that can increase cost. Utilizing the AWS Simple Monthly Calculator will also help you understand how some services should be multiplied to assure effective deployment of services as well as lower downtime. Furthermore, your enterprise will need to schedule services that can be automated to govern cost and monitor services so the enterprise is not overcharged. Keep in mind that without deploying an analysis to compile data regarding monthly cost, your enterprise could be victimized with increased spending without the necessity.

# Total Cost of Ownership Analysis

The TCO management tool is an essential way to approve investments that need to align with IT operational efficiency objectives and business performance needs. This includes gaining understanding on direct and indirect costs. Direct costs are costs directly accountable to a cost object (such as a particular project, facility, function, or product). These costs can be calculated with information from the accounting department, which can supply invoices, purchase orders, and payments. Additional direct costs include hardware and software, including the server, software licenses, maintenance contracts, and warranties [³]. Indirect costs (soft costs) are a little challenging to calculate. The biggest area for indirect costs includes considering what happens once the system goes down and how this downtime can impact productivity for both employees and customers. Calculating indirect costs requires viewing log files that calculate downtime for servers and multiplying those hours by an hourly rate your enterprise determines.

"TCO focuses on financial inputs and outputs. It does not account for business benefits and value that may be derived from the cloud, such as increased scalability, flexibility, and more opportunities for sharing and collaboration across geographic locations. Remember that when conducting TCO and other similar analysis, planning for cloud should not be only cost-focused but consider nonfinancial benefits as well" [⁴].

# Disaster Recovery and Backup

Conducting a price calculation for disaster recovery and backup for BallotOnline required utilizing AWS Elastic Disaster Recovery. This application enables your enterprise to reduce downtime and data loss with increased response rates and reliable recovery of on-premises and cloud-based applications, utilizing affordable storage, minimal compute, and point-in-time recovery. AWS RDS is billed hourly, per replicating server. However, there is a 25% average change rate.

# Return-on-Investment Analysis

The data and use cases your enterprise relies on will commonly mirror those BallotOnline utilizes, that is, website, messaging, disaster recovery and backup, and IT service planning. Thus, provided are examples of the calculated TCO monthly cost for the BallotOnline use case. Having this information will help you determine the return on investment (ROI) for each use case your enterprise considers utilizing. Otherwise, your enterprise will be entangled in cost of services for use cases that are not required and may create system vulnerabilities if not effectively secured.

- **Website use case**

  Amazon Lightsail virtual private server enables your enterprise to build an application or website. The monthly cost for BallotOnline was $245.77. This amount covered cost for three servers with a Linux operating system. Configurations for the application usage will differ tremendously from the service usage cost for BallotOnline. However, having knowledge of the system configuration settings will help you understand how important it is to assess cost of services. Take, for instance, the bundle for BallotOnline was configured for 0.05 GB and the enterprise Instance storage was configured for 20 GB, vPCU1, and the memory was set at 0.05 GB and 1 TB of data transfer quota. The server utilization was configured for 730 hours/month, which cost $10.29. Total annual estimate cost was $2,949.28. Figure 5-10 provides proof of concept.

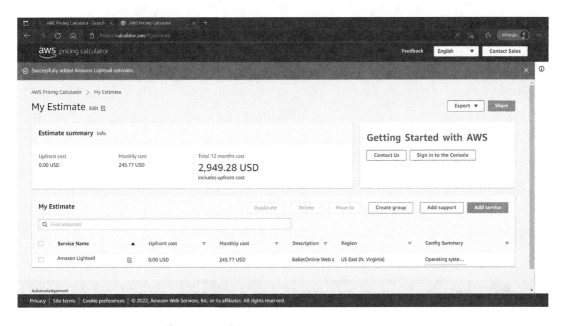

***Figure 5-10.***  *Estimated 12 month cost*

The ROI for the BallotOnline website was configured as follows:

Cost of initial (COI) investment $3,000 monthly × 5 years= $15,000

Gain from investment at 10%= $1500.00 | 20%= $3000.00 | 30%= $4500.00 | 40%= $6000.00 | 50%= $7500.00

Thus, the calculated ROI ranges from 10% to 50%. This calculated range of cost will be applied to each use case.

- **Messaging**

  Amazon Simple Notification Service is a highly available, durable, secure, fully managed pub/sub messaging service that enables your enterprise to decouple microservices and distributed systems and deploy serverless applications. AWS delivers 1 million message requests free under its free tier application. For BallotOnline the cost was estimated beyond this free tier at $21.29 per month. For 12 months the total cost was $255.48. Figure 5-11 provides proof of concept.

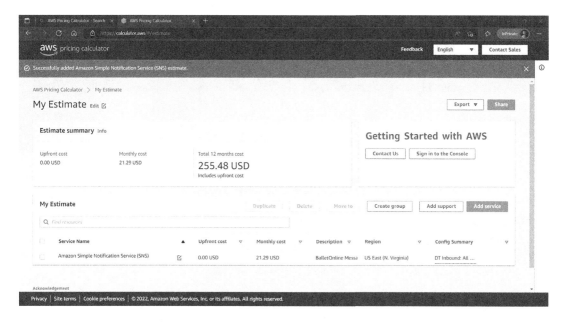

***Figure 5-11.** Proof of concept*

The ROI for BallotOnline messaging services totaled $255.48 for 12 months.

Cost of initial (COI) investment $21.29 × 12 months × 5 years= $1,277.40

Gain from investment at 10%=25.548 | 20%= 51.096 | 30%= 76.644 | 40%= 102.192 | 50%= 127.74.

- **Disaster recovery and backup**

   Configurations for BallotOnline were set for 5 GB for three servers with a monthly cost of $60.29. Figure 5-12 shows a proof of cost concept of $747.48.

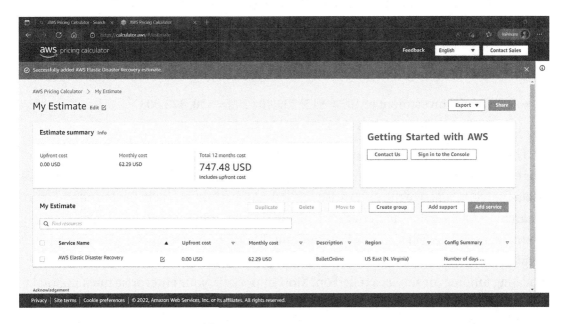

***Figure 5-12.*** *Estimated summary*

   The ROI for BallotOnline disaster recovery and backup totaled $747.48 for 12 months of service.

   Cost of initial investment $62.29 × 12 months × 5 years= $3,737.40

   Gain from investment at 10%= $373.74 | 20%= $747.48 | 30%= $1, 121.22 | 40%= $1, 494.96 | 50%= $1, 868.70

- **IT service plan**

   AWS CloudWatch was elected to monitor and manage services. This application provides data and actionable insights regarding AWS hybrid and on-premises applications as well as infrastructure resources. Thus, configurations were set at 100 metrics totaling $30.00 monthly. API metrics were set for 1,000,000 equaling $40.00 monthly. Log was set at 1,000 GB. In addition, when I elected to

151

store archival logs, configuration was set at 10,000 GB for logs delivered to S3. Monthly log watch cost was estimated at $12,590 with a total cost of $151,080 annually. The CloudWatch dashboard and alarms total cost was $37.00 monthly. Thus, the total cost for the IT service plan for BallotOnline with AWS is $152,364 annually. The ROI for BallotOnline IT service plan totaling at $152,364 for a 12-month service considers

Cost of initial investment $152,364 × 5 years= $761,820

Gain of investment at 10%= $15, 236.40 | 20%= $30, 472.80 | 30%= $45, 709.20 | 40%=$60,945.60 | 50%= $76,182.00

Thus, conducting a return-on-investment analysis is a positive investment to enable your enterprise to continue improving and upgrading usage of AWS services for each use case required to manage the enterprise services. As a result, you will need to continue researching AWS services to better understand the monthly cost for each use case your enterprise uses. You will also need to continue sharing research reports with executive members and stakeholders so they can have input in determining the use cases and allocating funding for services relied on. Most important, your enterprise must maintain ongoing communication with AWS support services to stay current with trends in system modifications and updates. Doing so will enable the enterprise to decrease system downtime cost and reduce unnecessary spending.

# Summary

Although your enterprise is implementing an effective strategy to prepare for cloud migration, orchestration, and automation, defining a clearly developed AWS Service Catalog that shares policy and compliance regulations governing each product the enterprise utilizes is important. To achieve this effectively, managing a monthly cost analysis will enable your enterprise to improve budget management, assess cost for each use case, and reduce liabilities. Integrating a total of cost ownership analysis will help the enterprise increase usage of constraints against security breach vulnerabilities and human error, and creating a return-on-investment analysis will help the enterprise understand the significance of investing in technology. Understanding both direct and indirect costs will reduce excess spending while increasing ROI and enterprise profitability.

# Discussion Questions

1). What is the total cost of ownership analysis?

2). What is a use case?

3). What does Amazon Service Catalog support?

4). What IT services can your enterprise control?

5). Why is the AWS Simple Monthly Calculator important?

6). How many questions do you need to answer when calculating AWS Directory Service Instances?

7). What are the top nine service applications provided by AWS?

8). How many custom metric categories are there with Amazon CloudWatch?

9). What does the AWS Solution Calculator total?

10). What does the TCO management tool offer?

# Notes

Introduction

AWS total cost of ownership calculator. (2022). Retrieved from `https://calculator.aws/#/`

Chapter 1

NIST SP 800-144 Guidelines on Security and Privacy in Public Cloud Computing. Retrieved from SP 800-144 Guidelines on Security and Privacy in Public Cloud Computing | CSRC (nist.gov)

NIST SP 800-181 Workforce Framework for Cybersecurity (NICE Framework). Retrieved from SP 800-181 Rev.1 Workforce Framework for Cybersecurity (NICE Framework) | CSRC (nist.gov)

Chapter 2

NIST SP 800-144 Guidelines on Security and Privacy in Public Cloud Computing. Retrieved from SP 800-144 Guidelines on Security and Privacy in Public Cloud Computing | CSRC (nist.gov)

NIST SP 500-291 Cloud Computing Standards Roadmap. Retrieved from NIST-SP 500-291 NIST Cloud Computing Standards Roadmap | NIST

Chapter 3

NIST SP 500-291 Cloud Computing Standards Roadmap. Retrieved from NIST-SP 500-291 NIST Cloud Computing Standards Roadmap | NIST

NIST SP 800-144 Guidelines on Security and Privacy in Public Cloud Computing. Retrieved from SP 800-144 Guidelines on Security and Privacy in Public Cloud Computing | CSRC (nist.gov)

NIST SP 800-210 General Access Control Guidance for Cloud Systems. Retrieved from SP 800-210 General Access Control Guidance for Cloud Systems | CSRC (nist.gov)

NIST SP 800-146 Cloud Computing Synopsis and Recommendations. Retrieved from SP 800-146 Cloud Computing Synopsis and Recommendations | CSRC (nist.gov)

AWS Podcast: Migration and Modernization. Retrieved from Migration and Modernization | AWS Executive Insights (amazon.com)

© Bradley Fowler 2023
B. Fowler, *AWS for Public and Private Sectors*, https://doi.org/10.1007/978-1-4842-9048-4

# Glossary

**access control list** – Helps enterprises manage access to buckets and objects acquired through AWS vender services.

**Application Programming Interface** – A system of tools and resources enveloped in an operating system that supports developers who create software applications.

**auditing** – Assessing a system for compliance, performance measurements, and security vulnerabilities and threats.

**audit tracking** – Enables verification of sequenced tasks and actions deployed as part of a process or operation.

**authentication** – Verifying the identity of a user and/or process.

**auto-scaling** – A method that adjusts the allocated number of computational resources hosted in a server, based on the load of measurements.

**AWS Glacier** – Low-cost cloud storage service for data that has longer retrieval timelines and is available through Amazon Web Services.

**AWS S3** – Object storage service that provides scalability, data availability, security, and effective performance.

**AWS Service Catalog** – Helps organizations centrally manage deployed IT services as well as helps organizations continue achieving consistent governance that is compliant.

**Central Processing Unit** – Key component of the computer operating system enveloping the primary memory and control unit. Contained in the microprocessor as an integrated circuit chip.

**CIA triad** – Confidentiality, integrity, and availability enacted as standards for computer security.

**CIDR notation** _– Compact representation of an IP address and all associated network masks.

**Cloud API** – Software that enables developers to connect cloud computing resources and services.

**Cloud Development Kit** (CDK) – Open source software development framework that defines an enterprise cloud application resource integrated with programming languages.

157

© Bradley Fowler 2023
B. Fowler, *AWS for Public and Private Sectors*, https://doi.org/10.1007/978-1-4842-9048-4

**cloud ecosystem** – A system of interdependent components working in partnership to provide cloud services.

**cloud command line interface** – Helps manage an enterprise AWS service including controlling multiple services using the command line through scripting languages.

**constraint rules** – Enterprise configuration regulations utilized to include and exclude, recommend, replace, and validate a product or set of products defined by other products or set of products placed in a cart.

**cyber-attacks** – Unwanted vicious acts deployed to invade and disrupt computer systems, software, and hardware.

**data packets** – Unit of data developed into a single packet that travels across a network path. Utilized in Internet Protocol transmission for data controlling the Web as well as other types of networks.

**decryption –** Processes encrypted data into its original format.

**encryption** – Converting an original message into a secure nonreadable format that protects the data at rest and in transmission.

**functional requirements** – Define the function of a system and its components.

**GDPR** – General Data Protection Regulation enacted by the European Union and the European Economic Area. A component of the EU law on privacy and human rights.

**Internet Protocol** – Set of rules for routing and addressing packets of data so the data can travel across the network and arrive at its correct destination.

**IP address** – Numerical representation that identifies a specific interface on a network.

**IP routing** – Method that transmits packets from a host on one end of a network to another host on a different remote network.

**latency** – A delay prior to data transferring. This expression conveys the amount of time taken for a data packet to travel from one network to another.

**load balancing** – Process of distributing tasks across a set of resources to increase efficiency.

**network engineering** – Maintaining the connectivity of an enterprise network including data, voice, calls, video, and wireless network services.

**open networking** – An open source network business model designed to promote networking through software-defined networking and standardization.

**Porter's Five Force Model** – A method of analyzing the operational environment of a competition of a business.

**ransomware** – Malware developed to take hostage of a victim's computer, hardware, and software, to hold for a ransom payment.

# References

Introduction

[1] National Institute of Science and Technology. (2021). "Managing Risk in the Cloud." Retrieved from `https://tsapps.nist.gov/publication/get_pdf.cfm?pub_id=919234`

[2] Amazon Web Services. (2022). AWS OpsWorks for Chef Automate. `https://aws.amazon.com/opsworks/chefautomate/`

Chapter 1

[1] Amazon Web Services. (2022). AWS Pricing/TCO Tools. Retrieved from `https://doc.aws.amazon.com/whitepapers/latest/how-aws-pricing/works/aws-pricingtco-tools.html`

[2] Piccoli, G. & Pigni, F. (2020). *Information Systems for Managers: With Cases.* (4th Ed). Prospect Press, Burlington, VT.

[3] NIST.gov. (2021). "Managing Risk in the Cloud." Retrieved from `https://tsapps.nist.gov/publication/get_pdf.cfm?pub_id=919234`

[4] vmware.com. (n.d.). Cloud Computing Architecture. Retrieved from `www.vmware.com/topics/glossary/content/cloud-computing-infrastructure`

[5] ISO/IEC 27001:2013. (2013). Information technology – security techniques – information security management systems – requirements. `www.iso.org/obp/ui/#iso:std:iso-iec:27001:ed-2:v1:en`

[6] National Security Agency. (2021). Mitigating Cloud Vulnerabilities. Retrieved from `https://media.defense.gov/2020/Jan/22/2002237484/-1/-1/0/CSI-MITIGATING-CLOUD-VULNERABILITIES_20200121.PDF`

[7] Ibid.

© Bradley Fowler 2023
B. Fowler, *AWS for Public and Private Sectors*, https://doi.org/10.1007/978-1-4842-9048-4

[8] Hashizume, K., Rosado, D. G., Fernandez-Medina, E., & Fernandez, E. B. (2013). *Journal of Internet Services and Applications*. Retrieved from `https://jisajournal.springeropen.com/articles/10.1186/1869-0238-4-5`

[9] De Filippi, P., & Vieira, M. S. (2013). "The Commodification of Information Commons." In *International Journal of the Commons*, Special Issue: The Knowledge Commons: from historical open science to digitally integrated research networks.

[10] Weins, K. (2017). Cloud computing trends: 2017 state of the cloud survey [Blog post]. Retrieved from `www.rightscale.com/blog/cloud-industry-insights/cloud-computing-trends-2017-state-cloud-survey`

[11] Liu, F., Tong, J., Mao, J., Bohn, R., Messina, J., Badger, L., & Leaf, D. (2011). Special publication 500-292: National Institute of Standards and Technology (NIST) cloud computing reference architecture. Retrieved from `www.nist.gov/publications/nist-cloud-computing-reference-architecture`

[12] Schilling, M. (2020). *Strategic Management of Technological Innovation*. (6th Ed). McGraw Hill, New York, NY, p. 123.

[13] Ibid.

[14] Ibid.

[15] InformationWeek.com. (2018). Commentary. Retrieved from `www.informationweek.com/cloud/aws-vs-azure-users-share-their-experiences/a/d-id/1332752`

[16] CloudHeath. (2021). CloudHealth Tech Staff. Retrieved from `www.cloudhealthtech.com/blog/azure-vs-aws-pricing`

[17] Hashizume, K., Rosado, D. G., Fernandez-Medina E., & Fernandez, E. B. (2013). *Journal of Internet Services and Applications*. Retrieved from `https://leocontent.umgc.edu/content/dam/course-content/tgs/cca/cca-610/document/AnAnalysisofSecurityIssuesForCloudComputing_checked.pdf?ou=546563`

Chapter 2

[1] Massachusetts Institute of Technology. (1999). Internetworking Technology Overview. Retrieved from http://fab.cba.mit.edu/classes/961.04/people/neil/ip.pdf

[2] Ibid.

[3] Morley, D. & Parker, C. S. (2007). *Understanding Computers.* (11th Ed). Thomas Course Technology, Boston, MA, p. 294.

[4] Ibid.

[5] Amazon Web Services. (2021). What is DNS? Retrieved from https://aws.amazon.com/route53/what-is-dns/

[6] Ibid.

[7] Ibid.

[8] Janssen, D. (2020). 8 Steps to Understanding IP Subnetting. Retrieved from www.techopedia.com/6/28587/internet/8-steps-to-understanding-ip-subnetting

[9] Guru99.com. (n.d.). IP Address Classes. Retrieved from www.guru99.com/ip-address-classes.html

[10] Ibid.

[11] Both, D. (2016). A Linux Networking Guide to CIDR Notation and Configuration. Retrieved from https://opensource.com/article/16/12/cidr-network-notation-configuration-linux

[12] Ibid.

[13] Morley, D. & Parker, C. S. (2007). *Understanding Computers.* (11th Ed). Thomas Course Technology, Boston, MA, p. 294.

[14] Cloudflare.com. (n.d.). What is Network as a Service? Retrieved from www.cloudflare.com/learning/network-layer/network-as-a-service-naas/

[15] IBM.com. (n.d.). TCP Flow Control and the Sliding Window. Retrieved from www.ibm.com/docs/en/spectrum-protect/8.1.9?topic=tuning-tcp-flow-control

[16] Ibid.

[17] Ma, C. (2014). SDN Secrets of Amazon and Google. Retrieved from www.infoworld.com/article/2608106/sdn-secrets-of-amazon-and-google.html

[18] Ibid.

[19] Foresta, F. (2017). University of Bologna. Integration of SDN Frameworks and Cloud Computing Platforms. Retrieved from https://amslaurea.unibo.it/14271/1/ForestaFrancescoMasterThesis.pdf

[20] Stallings, W. (2013). *The Internet Protocol Journal*. Retrieved from http://ipj.dreamhosters.com/wp-content/uploads/issues/2013/ipj16-1.pdf

[21] Amazon Web Services. (2021). How Amazon VPC Works? Retrieved from https://docs.aws.amazon.com/vpc/latest/userguide/how-it-works.html

[22] Ibid.

[23] Ibid.

[24] Davis, B. (2019). What Are the Advantages of Using a Command Line vs. a GUI? Retrieved from www.mvorganizing.org/what-are-the-advantages-of-using-a-command-line-vs-a-gui/

[25] Puvvula, W. D. (2021). Deep Dive on AWS CloudFormation Macros to Transform Your Templates. Retrieved from https://aws.amazon.com/blogs/mt/deep-dive-on-aws-cloudformation-macros-to-transform-your-templates/

[26] Ibid.

[27] Ibid.

[28] AlliedTelecom.net. (2021). How the Cloud Can Improve Business Communications. Retrieved from www.alliedtelecom.net/cloud-can-improve-business-communications/

Chapter 3

[1] Amazon Web Services. (2020). SQL Server Database Migration Strategies. Retrieved from `https://docs.aws.amazon.com/prescriptive-guidance/latest/migration-sql-server/strategies.html`

[2] Amazon Web Services. (2020). AWS Application Discovery Service. Retrieved from `https://docs.aws.amazon.com/application-discovery/latest/userguide/appdiscovery-ug.pdf#what-is-appdiscovery`

[3] Ibid.

[4] Ibid.

[5] Ibid.

[6] Ibid.

[7] Ibid.

[8] Government Accountability Office. (2011). Federal Guidance for Implementing Cloud Computing. Retrieved from GAO-10-513 Information Security: Federal Guidance Needed to Address Control Issues with Implementing Cloud Computing.

[9] Ibid.

[10] Ibid.

[11] AWS.com. (2022). Database Migrations. Retrieved from `https://aws.amazon.com/products/databases/migrations/`

[12] Roberts, S. (2021). New Strategy Recommendations Service Helps Streamline AWS Cloud Migration and Modernization. Retrieved from `https://aws.amazon.com/blogs/aws/new-strategy-recommendations-service-helps-streamline-aws-cloud-migration-and-modernization/`

[13] AWS.com. (2016). AWS Database Migration Service. p. 83. Retrieved from `https://aws.amazon.com/dms/`

[14] Ibid.

[15] Ibid.

[16] Ibid.

[17] AWS.com (2022). AWS Systems Manager. Seattle, WA. p. 1. Retrieved from `https://docs.aws.amazon.com/systems-manager/latest/userguide/systems-manager-ug.pdf#what-is-systems-manager`

[18] Ibid.

[19] Ibid.

Chapter 4

[1] Loutas, N., Kamateri, E., Bosi, F., & Tarabanis, K. A. (2011). Cloud computing interoperability: The state of play. In *IEEE Third International Conference on Cloud Computing Technology and Science (CloudCom)*, 752–757.

[2] Hosken, M. (2020). VMware.com Cloud Exit Planning. Retrieved from `https://blogs.vmware.com/cloud/2020/12/18/cloud-exit-planning-building-future-proofed-multi-cloud-strategy-part-one-two/`

[3] Schiemann, W. (2020). Cloud Exit Strategy: Ensure Compliance and Prevent Vendor Lock-In. Retrieved from `www.meshcloud.io/2020/06/18/cloud-exit-strategy-ensure-compliance-and-prevent-vendor-lock-in/`

[4] AWS.com. (2021). Performance Efficiency in AWS Multi-Tenant SaaS Environments. Retrieved from `https://aws.amazon.com/blogs/apn/performance-efficiency-in-aws-multi-tenant-saas-environments/`

[5] Ibid.

[6] AWS.com. (2021). AWS Cloud developer Kit (CDK) Developer Guide. Why Use the AWS CDK? Retrieved from `https://docs.aws.amazon.com/cdk/latest/guide/awscdk.pdf#home`

[7] Ibid.

[8] Ibid.

[9] Ibid.

[10] Linksys.com. (2021). Differences Between IPV4 and IPV6. Retrieved from `https://bit.ly/3BTKCLB`

[11] AWS.com (2021). Commvault Cloud Architecture Guide for Amazon Web Services. Retrieved from `https://kapost-files-prod.s3.amazonaws.com/published/55db3030f2af23b1 2f000632/commvault-cloud-architecture-guide-for-aws.pdf? kui=-3lGybvyOfTpsIlDEJXAdQ`

[12] Ibid.

[13] Ibid.

[14] Ibid.

[15] AWS CloudWatch. (2021). Creating a CloudWatch Dashboard. Retrieved from `https://docs.aws.amazon.com/ AmazonCloudWatch/latest/monitoring/acw-ug.pdf#create_ dashboard`

[16] Ibid.

[17] AWS.com. (2021). Amazon Simple Storage Service. Retrieved from `https://docs.aws.amazon.com/AmazonS3/latest/ userguide/s3-userguide.pdf#UsingBucket`

[18] NetApp.com. (2021). Cloud Sync Overview. Retrieved from `https://docs.netapp.com/us-en/occm/concept_cloud_ sync.html`

Chapter 5

[1] Amazon.com. (2022). AWS Simple Monthly Calculator. Retrieved from General SAP Guides – SAP Guides (amazon.com).

[2] Mullahy, T. (2022). Channel Future: Should You Use Multiple Cloud Providers for Disaster Recovery? Retrieved from Should You Use Multiple Cloud Providers for Disaster Recovery? – Channel Futures.

[3] Chan, M. (2016). Cost of cloud computing: How to calculate the true cost of moving to the cloud. Retrieved from `www.thorntech.com/2016/10/cost-of-cloud-computing-how-to-calculate-the-true-cost-of-moving-to-the-cloud/`

[4] Hill, R., Hirsch, L., Lake, P. & Moshiri, S. (2013). *Guide to Cloud Computing: Principles and Practice [Books24x7 version]*. Retrieved from `http://common.books24x7.com.ezproxy.umgc.edu/toc.aspx?bookid=76972`

# Index

## W, X

WebSocket APIs, 36

World Intellectual Property Organization
(WIPO), 11, 13

## Y, Z

YAML Ain't Markup Language
(YAML), 35, 141

Printed in the United States
by Baker & Taylor Publisher Services